Assessment of Soil-Gas, Soil, and Water Contamination at the Former Hospital Landfill, Fort Gordon, Georgia, 2009–2010

By W. Fred Falls, Andral W. Caldwell, Wladmir B. Guimaraes, W. Hagan Ratliff, John B. Wellborn, and James E. Landmeyer

Prepared in cooperation with the U.S. Department of the Army Environmental and Natural Resources Management Office of the U.S. Army Signal Center and Fort Gordon

Open-File Report 2011–1144

U.S. Department of the Interior
U.S. Geological Survey

U.S. Department of the Interior
KEN SALAZAR, Secretary

U.S. Geological Survey
Marcia K. McNutt, Director

U.S. Geological Survey, Reston, Virginia: 2011

For more information on the USGS—the Federal source for science about the Earth, its natural and living resources, natural hazards, and the environment, visit http://www.usgs.gov or call 1–888–ASK–USGS.

For an overview of USGS information products, including maps, imagery, and publications,
visit http://www.usgs.gov/pubprod

To order this and other USGS information products, visit http://store.usgs.gov

Contents

Abstract..1

Introduction...1

    Purpose and Scope 3

    Description of the Study Area 3

Methods...4

    Hyporheic-Zone and Soil-Gas Samplers 4

    Soil Samples 6

    Surface-Water Samples 8

Results 8

    Hyporheic-Zone Samplers 8

    Soil-Gas Samplers: July 26–30, 2010..8

    Soil-Gas Samplers: September 16–22, 2010 10

    Soil Samples 10

    Surface-Water Samples 14

Summary...14

References Cited..15

Figures

1.   Map showing approximate locations of Fort Gordon and the former hospital landfill study area at Fort Gordon, Richmond County, Georgia, 2009–2010....................................2

2.   Photographs of former hospital landfill study area characterized by trees and thick underbrush in the area of the passive soil-gas survey and thick underbrush on the flood plain adjacent to the hyporheic zone of the unnamed tributary to Butler Creek, Fort Gordon, Richmond County, Georgia, 2009–2010 3

3.   Photographs of geologic strata forming an outcrop and a waterfall on the unnamed tributary to Butler Creek adjacent to the former hospital landfill study area also could form local hydraulic confinement and affect the distribution of groundwater discharge to the creek, Fort Gordon, Richmond County, Georgia, 2009–2010....................................4

4.   Photographs of passive soil-gas sampler used in the hyporheic-zone and soil-gas study areas prior to deployment, and in an air-tight vial for shipment from and to the laboratory for analysis 4

5.   Photographs of an example of a hyporheic-zone sampler showing the vented stainless-steel drive point and cap used to house the passive soil-gas sampler and a deployed sampler inserted into the creek-bed sediments 5

6.   Photographs of installation of a passive soil-gas sampler in the landfill soil consisted of drilling a borehole in the soil with a stainless-steel drill bit attached to a cordless drill, attaching one end of a string to the soil-gas sampler and the other end to a cork plug, inserting the soil-gas sampler into the borehole, and sealing the borehole with the cork plug to keep out surface material and water...6

7.   Photographs of soil sample collected in the interval from land surface to a depth of 6 inches with a stainless-steel hand auger and transferred from the auger to a plastic container for shipment to the laboratory...7

8–12. Maps showing–

8. Locations and identification numbers of hyporheic-zone samplers along the unnamed tributary to Butler Creek, and total petroleum hydrocarbon concentrations in micrograms per liter for each sampler, April 9, 2010, and location of the surface-water sampling site, September 8, 2010, former hospital landfill, Fort Gordon, Georgia..7

9. Locations and identification numbers of passive soil-gas samplers, and ranges of soil-gas mass for total petroleum hydrocarbons in micrograms, former hospital landfill, Fort Gordon, Georgia, July 26–30, 2010..9

10. Locations and identification numbers of passive soil-gas samplers, and ranges of combined soil-gas mass for benzene, toluene, ethylbenzene, and xylene (BTEX gasoline compounds) in micrograms, former hospital landfill, Fort Gordon, Georgia, July 26–30, 2010..11

11. Locations and identification numbers of passive soil-gas samplers, and ranges of combined soil-gas mass for undecane, tridecane, and pentadecane (C_{11}, C_{13}, and C_{15}, diesel compounds) in micrograms, former hospital landfill, Fort Gordon, Georgia, July 26–30, 2010..12

12. Locations and identification numbers of September 2010 soil-gas samplers analyzed for volatile and semivolatile organic compounds classified as chemical warfare agents and explosives, August 30, 2010, and soil samples analyzed for inorganic constituents, former hospital landfill study area, Fort Gordon, Georgia 13

Tables (located at the back of the report)

1. Concentrations of volatile and semivolatile organic compounds detected in the passive soil-gas samplers deployed and collected in the water-saturated hyporheic zone of an unnamed tributary of Butler Creek adjacent to the former hospital landfill, Fort Gordon, Georgia, April 9, 2010. 17

2. Mass of volatile and semivolatile organic compounds detected in passive soil-gas samplers deployed and recovered in the soil of the former hospital landfill, Fort Gordon, Georgia, July 26-30, 2010...19

3. Mass of chemical agents and explosives classified as volatile and semivolatile organic compounds detected in passive soil-gas samples deployed and collected in the soil of the former hospital landfill, Fort Gordon, Georgia, September 16-22, 2010...28

4. Inorganic constituents detected in soil samples 1 – 5 collected from land surface to a depth of 6 inches at the former hospital landfill, Fort Gordon, Georgia, August 30, 2010..30

5. Field parameters and analytical results for an unfiltered surface-water sample collected from the unnamed tributary to Butler Creek adjacent to the former hospital landfill, Fort Gordon, Georgia, September 8, 2010...31

Conversion Factors

Inch/Pound to SI

Multiply	By	To obtain
	Length	
inch (in.)	2.54	centimeter (cm)
inch (in.)	25.4	millimeter (mm)
foot (ft)	0.3048	meter (m)
mile (mi)	1.609	kilometer (km)
	Area	
acre	4,047	square meter (m^2)
acre	0.4047	hectare (ha)
acre	0.4047	square hectometer (hm^2)
acre	0.004047	square kilometer (km^2)

Horizontal coordinate information is referred to the North American Datum of 1983 (NAD 83).

Water quality, soil-gas, and soil units

μg	microgram
μg/g	microgram per gram
μg/L	microgram per liter
μg/kg	microgram per kilogram
mL	milliliter

Selected acronyms and abbreviations used in this report:

bdl	Below detection level
BTEX	Benzene, toluene, ethylbenzene, and xylene (total)
C_{11}, C_{13}, C_{15}	Undecane, tridecane, and pentadecane (total)
GC/MS	Gas chromatography/mass spectroscopy
ICP-MS	Inductively Coupled Plasma-Mass Spectrometry
MDL	Method detection level
MTBE	Methyl *tert*-butyl ether
PAH	Polycyclic aromatic hydrocarbon
PCE	Perchloroethene (also known as perchloroethylene and tetrachloroethene)
RCRA	Resource Conservation and Recovery Act
RSL	Regional Screening Level
SCDHEC	South Carolina Department of Health and Environmental Control
SVOC	Semivolatile organic compound
TCE	Trichloroethene (also known as trichloroethylene)
TPH	Total Petroleum Hydrocarbons
USEPA	U.S. Environmental Protection Agency
USGS	U.S. Geological Survey
VOC	Volatile organic compound

Assessment of Soil-Gas, Soil and Water Contamination at the Former Hospital Landfill, Fort Gordon, Georgia, 2009–2010

By W. Fred Falls,[1] Andral W. Caldwell,[1] Wladmir B. Guimaraes,[1] W. Hagan Ratliff,[2] John B. Wellborn,[3] and James E. Landmeyer[1]

Abstract

Soil gas, soil, and water were assessed for organic and inorganic constituents at the former hospital landfill located in a 75-acre study area near the Dwight D. Eisenhower Army Medical Center, Fort Gordon, Georgia, from April to September 2010. Passive soil-gas samplers were analyzed to evaluate organic constituents in the hyporheic zone of a creek adjacent to the landfill and soil gas within the estimated boundaries of the former landfill. Soil and water samples were analyzed to evaluate inorganic constituents in soil samples, and organic and inorganic constituents in the surface water of a creek adjacent to the landfill, respectively. This assessment was conducted to provide environmental constituent data to Fort Gordon pursuant to requirements of the Resource Conservation and Recovery Act Part B Hazardous Waste Permit process.

Results from the hyporheic-zone assessment in the unnamed tributary adjacent to the study area indicated that total petroleum hydrocarbons and octane were the most frequently detected organic compounds in groundwater beneath the creek bed. The highest concentrations for these compounds were detected in the upstream samplers of the hyporheic-zone study area.

The effort to delineate landfill activity in the study area focused on the western 14 acres of the 75-acre study area where the hyporheic-zone study identified the highest concentrations of organic compounds. This also is the part of the study area where a debris field also was identified in the southern part of the 14 acres. The southern part of this 14-acre study area, including the debris field, is steeper and not as heavily wooded, compared to the central and northern parts.

Fifty-two soil-gas samplers were used for the July 2010 soil-gas survey in the 14-acre study area and mostly detected total petroleum hydrocarbons, and gasoline and diesel compounds. The highest soil-gas masses for total petroleum hydrocarbons, diesel compounds, and the only valid detection of perchloroethene were in the southern part of the study area to the west of the debris field. However, all other detections of total petroleum hydrocarbons greater than 10 micrograms and diesel greater than 0.04 micrograms, and all detections of the combined mass of benzene, toluene, ethylbenzene, and xylene were found down slope from the debris field in the central and northern parts of the study area.

Five soil-gas samplers were deployed and recovered from September 16 to 22, 2010, and were analyzed for organic compounds classified as chemical agents or explosives. Chloroacetophenones (a tear gas component) were the only compounds detected above a method detection level and were detected at the same location as the highest total petroleum hydrocarbons and diesel detections in the southern part of the 14-acre study area.

Composite soil samples collected at five locations were analyzed for 35 inorganic constituents. None of the inorganic constituents exceeded the regional screening levels. One surface-water sample collected in the western end of the hyporheic-zone study area had a trichlorofluoromethane concentration above the laboratory reporting level and estimated concentrations of chloroform, fluoranthene, and isophorone below laboratory reporting levels.

Introduction

Fort Gordon is a U.S. Department of the Army facility located in east-central Georgia, approximately 10 miles southwest of Augusta, Georgia (fig. 1). A cantonment (military housing) area is located in the northeastern part of Fort

[1]U.S. Geological Survey, Columbia, South Carolina.

[2]Environmental Branch, Fort Gordon, Georgia.

[3]Environmental and Natural Resources, Fort Gordon, Georgia.

Gordon. Part of the cantonment area consists of an abandoned landfill near the Dwight D. Eisenhower Army Medical Center, known as the former hospital landfill (the landfill). The landfill was located on the southern bank of an unnamed tributary to Butler Creek but the exact boundaries and materials disposed of within the landfill are unknown.

Because the effects of past activities at the landfill on environmental resources were unknown, an assessment was conducted to provide screening-level environmental

contamination data to Fort Gordon personnel to comply with the requirements of the Resource Conservation and Recovery Act (RCRA) Part B Hazardous Waste Permit process. An initial investigation to assess potential environmental effects is warranted because the landfill is located in the outcrop area of the Dublin and Midville aquifer systems, which are used for drinking water by the towns of Augusta and Hephzibah (Williams, 2007).

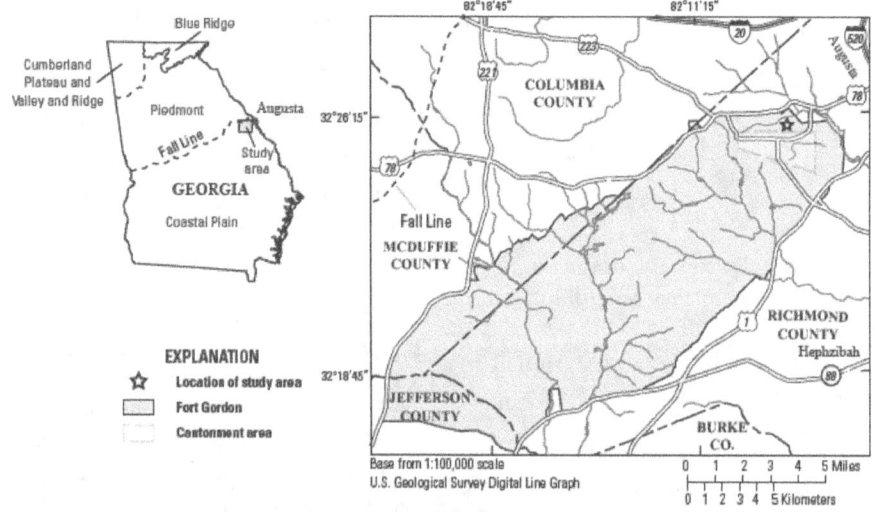

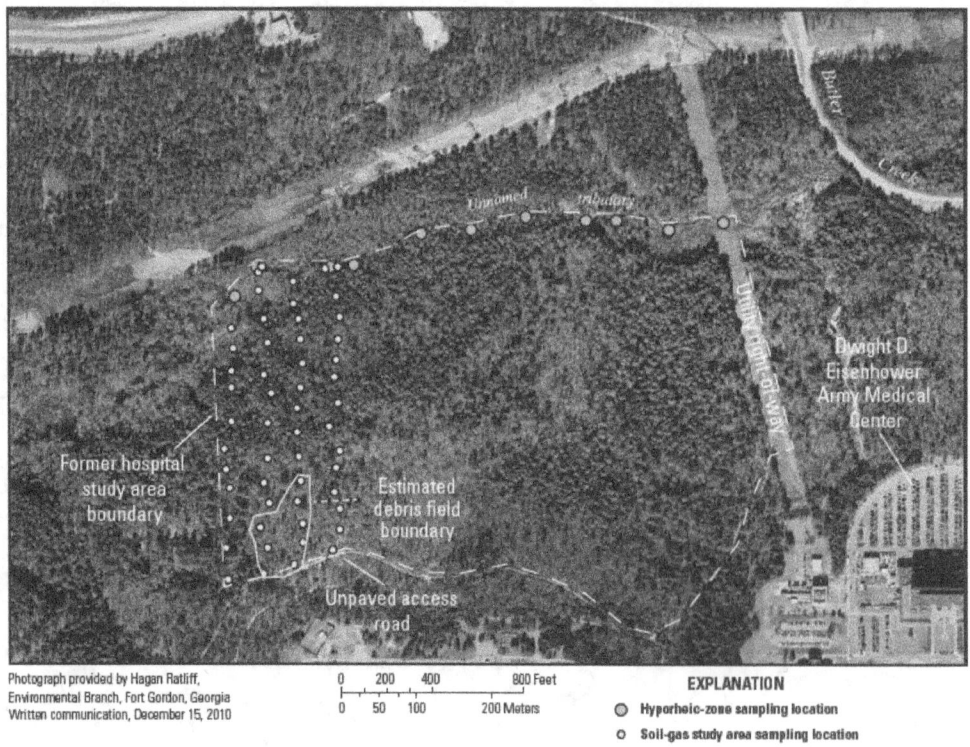

Figure 1. Approximate locations of Fort Gordon and the former hospital landfill study area at Fort Gordon, Richmond County, Georgia, 2009–2010.

Purpose and Scope

The U.S. Geological Survey, in cooperation with the U.S. Department of the Army Environmental and Natural Resources Management Office of the U.S. Army Signal Center and Fort Gordon, Georgia, assessed soil gas, soil, and water for contaminants at the former hospital landfill and the adjacent segment of an unnamed tributary to Butler Creek from April to September 2010. The site assessment was conducted to provide environmental constituent data and consisted of (a) a preliminary survey along the unnamed tributary to Butler Creek to identify potential areas of volatile and semivolatile organic compounds (VOC and SVOC) in water from the hyporheic zone adjacent to the landfill, (b) two soil-gas surveys for VOCs and SVOCs and soil samples for inorganic constituents in the landfill, and (c) collection of surface water for organic and inorganic compounds from the adjacent segment of the unnamed tributary. This report describes the results of the analyses of these samples and includes maps showing the locations of the more frequent detections identified in the study area.

Description of the Study Area

Fort Gordon is located south of the Fall Line in the northern part of the Coastal Plain Physiographic Province near Augusta, Georgia (fig. 1). Fort Gordon is underlain by Cretaceous and Tertiary strata and is characterized by surficial soils and sediments of unconsolidated sands, semiconsolidated sandstones, and layers of clay that include kaolinite (Hetrick, 1992; Gregory and others, 2001).

The study area for the former hospital landfill is located in the northern part of the cantonment area and includes approximately 75 acres between an unnamed tributary to Butler Creek and an unpaved access road south of the tributary (fig. 1). A utility (power) right-of-way was chosen as the eastern boundary of the study area. The western boundary was estimated to be 2,200 feet (ft) west of the utility right-of-way. The landfill was assumed to be approximately 1.5 acres (John B. Wellborn, Environmental and Natural Resources Division, Fort Gordon, Georgia, written commun., 2009). The landfill was used from the 1960s through the 1970s for waste disposal, but the exact location and the contents of the landfill are unknown.

Most of the landfill study area is characterized as a sandy slope with a stand of pines and hardwoods, and thick underbrush in places (fig. 2A). The unpaved access road along the southern boundary of the study area is still accessible and is presently (2011) being used for military training exercises (fig. 1). A few unpaved access roads also were identified in the study area during site visits in 2009 and 2010, but the roads generally were overgrown with vegetation and were only accessible on foot. Disturbed soil conditions and the presence of surficial debris (asphalt, bricks, and wood) observed in the southwestern corner of the study area during site visits in

2009 and 2010 indicated that this area may have been used for waste-disposal activities in the past (fig. 1). Except for previously mentioned features, there is no evidence of manmade structures in the present-day (2011) study area.

The banks and flood plain of the unnamed tributary also are wooded and covered in thick underbrush in places (fig. 2B). Geologic strata crop out along the creek bank in the western part of the hyporheic-zone study area (fig. 3A). The clay strata are more resistant to erosion and locally form waterfalls in the western end of the study area (fig. 3B). These clay strata also could form local hydraulic confinement in the water table beneath the western end of the study area and, if so, could affect the discharge of contaminated groundwater to the hyporheic zone of the unnamed tributary.

Figure 2.   Former hospital landfill study area characterized by (A) trees and thick underbrush in the area of the passive soil-gas survey and (B) thick underbrush on the flood plain adjacent to the hyporheic zone of the unnamed tributary to Butler Creek, Fort Gordon, Richmond County, Georgia, 2009–2010.

Figure 3. Geologic strata forming (*A*) an outcrop and (*B*) a waterfall on the unnamed tributary to Butler Creek adjacent to the former hospital landfill study area also could form local hydraulic confinement and affect the distribution of groundwater discharge to the creek, Fort Gordon, Richmond County, Georgia, 2009–2010.

Methods

Samples collected for the purposes of this study were collected and analyzed using standard field and laboratory methods (U.S. Environmental Protection Agency 1998, 2006; U.S. Geological Survey National Field Manual, variously dated). The samples were collected for (a) assessments of potential areas of VOC/SVOC contamination in the water-saturated hyporheic zone of an unnamed tributary adjacent to the landfill, (b) VOC/SVOC contamination in the soil gas of the landfill, (c) inorganic contamination in the landfill soil, and (d) VOC/SVOC/inorganic contamination of the surface water in the unnamed tributary adjacent to the landfill under base-flow conditions.

Hyporheic-Zone and Soil-Gas Samplers

The assessments of organic compounds in the hyporheic zone of the unnamed tributary to Butler Creek on April 9, 2010, and the two passive soil-gas surveys from July 26 to 30, 2010, and September 16 to 22, 2010, in the landfill study area were conducted by using the GORE™ passive soil-gas sampler, a commercially available sampler that is based on GORE-TEX™ membrane technology (U.S. Environmental Protection Agency, 1998; W.L.Gore & Associates, Inc., 2004; American Society for Testing and Materials, 2006). The sampler consists of a proprietary adsorbent medium placed inside a shoestring-shaped GORE-TEX™ sleeve (fig. 4*A*). The passive soil-gas approach was approved for use at abandoned sites at Fort Gordon by the Hazardous Waste Management Branch, Georgia Environmental Protection Department (William Powell, P.E., Environmental Engineer, Department of Defense Remediation Unit, oral commun., 2008).

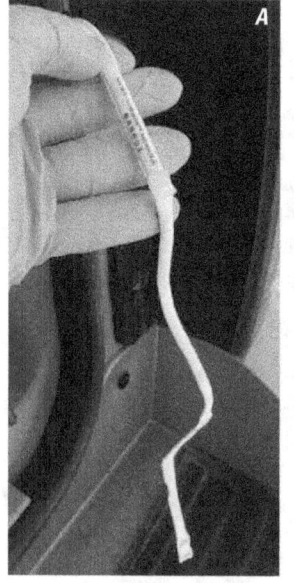

Figure 4. Passive soil-gas sampler used in the hyporheic-zone and soil-gas study areas (*A*) prior to deployment, and (*B*) in an air-tight vial for shipment from and to the laboratory for analysis.

The adsorbent medium inside the soil-gas samplers can adsorb a wide variety of VOCs and SVOCs, including solvents, such as trichloroethene (TCE) and perchloroethene (PCE; also known as tetrachloroethene); gasoline-range compounds, such as benzene, toluene, ethylbenzene, and xylenes (collectively referred to as BTEX); the gasoline additive methyl *tert*-butyl ether (MTBE); diesel-range compounds (collectively referred to as C_{11}, C_{13}, and C_{15}), such as undecane, tridecane, and pentadecane; and polycyclic aromatic hydrocarbons (PAHs), such as naphthalene. The

adsorbent medium also can adsorb organic compounds classified as chemical warfare agents, such as mustard gas and tear
gas, and explosives, including nitrobenzene and nitrotoluene
compounds.

Passive soil-gas results can indicate the presence of
particular organic compounds and are a rapid approach for
environmental assessment of organic compounds. The results
do not, however, reveal if the detection was derived from free
product, residual-phase compounds adsorbed on soil particles,
vapors in the unsaturated zone, or dissolved compounds in
shallow and deep groundwater (unless the sampler is deployed
in direct contact with water). In water deployments, such as
the hyporheic zone and the flood plain, organic vapors from
the dissolved compounds in the water can pass through the
GORE-TEX™ sleeve to adhere to the adsorbent medium, but
water, dissolved compounds, and sediment are excluded by
the sleeve. In unsaturated soil deployments, higher soil-gas
mass in a sample tends to be related to the presence of residual
compounds or free product that is close to the land surface
where the soil-gas sampler is located. If such source material
is located at greater depths, however, the soil-gas mass for
organic compounds generally will be lower. A lower value
near known sources may be caused by various attenuation
processes that affect the soil-gas mass prior to detection. In
both cases, however, the soil-gas samplers help to indicate the
presence or absence of organic constituents.

The soil-gas samplers used for direct water contact in
the hyporheic zone of the unnamed tributary were inserted in
vented, stainless-steel drive points and pushed by hand into the
water-saturated alluvial sediments of the creek bed to a depth
of 12 inches (in.; fig. 5). These soil-gas samplers, therefore,
were used to assess the presence of organic compounds in
groundwater near the point of discharge to the surface-water
system. The first sampler for the hyporheic-zone assessment
was deployed at a location assumed to be at or below the
downstream boundary of the study area. The remaining
samplers were deployed at 100- to 300-ft intervals along the
creek in an effort to locate the upstream limit of possible
contaminated groundwater discharge from the landfill to the
creek. The hyporheic-zone samplers were recovered after 2 to
3 hours of exposure to groundwater. Three trip blanks were
shipped to the laboratory with the environmental samplers for
quality control.

Soil-gas sampler locations for the soil-gas surveys in
the landfill study area were created with a stainless-steel bit
attached to a cordless drill (fig. 6). The bit was used to drill a
0.5 in.-diameter borehole in the soil to a depth of 15 in. The
depth of 15 in. was similar to the depth recommended by the
U.S. Environmental Protection Agency (USEPA) for soil-gas
investigations (U.S. Environmental Protection Agency,
1998). A string was attached to a cork plug at one end and the
sampler at the other end and was used to lower and suspend
the sampler in the borehole. The cork plug sealed the borehole
at land surface to prevent surface water and ambient land-
surface material from entering the borehole. The auger was

Figure 5. An example of a hyporheic-zone sampler showing
(*A*) the vented stainless-steel drive point and cap used to house
the passive soil-gas sampler and (*B*) a deployed sampler inserted
into the creek-bed sediments (the top of the deployed sampler
is attached to the submerged end of the pink string in the
photograph).

cleaned with a paper towel between boreholes. All soil-gas
samplers were recovered after 4 to 5 days.

Each soil-gas sampler recovered in the field was placed in
its original 20-milliliter air-tight vial and sent to the
commercial laboratory (W.L. Gore & Associates, Inc.) for
analysis (fig. 4*B*). A few of the samplers were kept in the
air-tight vials during the field deployment of environmental
samplers and were shipped back to the laboratory as trip
blanks.

All soil-gas samplers, including those deployed in the
unsaturated soil zone and water-saturated environments, were
processed and analyzed at the laboratory by using a modifica-
tion of USEPA method 8260/8270 (U.S. Environmental
Protection Agency, 2006). Prior to analysis, each sampler
was processed in an automated thermal desorption unit to
produce a gas sample of the VOCs and SVOCs adsorbed on
the sampler. The gas sample was analyzed by a gas chromato-
graph equipped with mass-selective detectors. The laboratory
analyzed instrument and method blanks for quality assurance,
in addition to trip blanks, and was in compliance with Good
Laboratory Practices and ISO Guide 25 (International Organization for Standardization, 1990). Results were expressed as
concentration (microgram per liter) for samplers deployed in
the water-saturated hyporheic zone of the unnamed tributary to
Butler Creek and as mass (micrograms) for soil-gas samplers
deployed in the unsaturated soil of the landfill. The results
for hyporheic-zone and soil-gas samples are presented in the
text and tables 1 to 3 as the unrounded values in the format
reported by the commercial laboratory.

The laboratory results provided screening-level data for
the assessment of 31 organic analytes. In addition, results of
individual compounds were summed to calculate values for
the combined masses (soil gas) or concentrations (water) of
benzene, toluene, ethylbenzene, and xylenes (gasoline-range

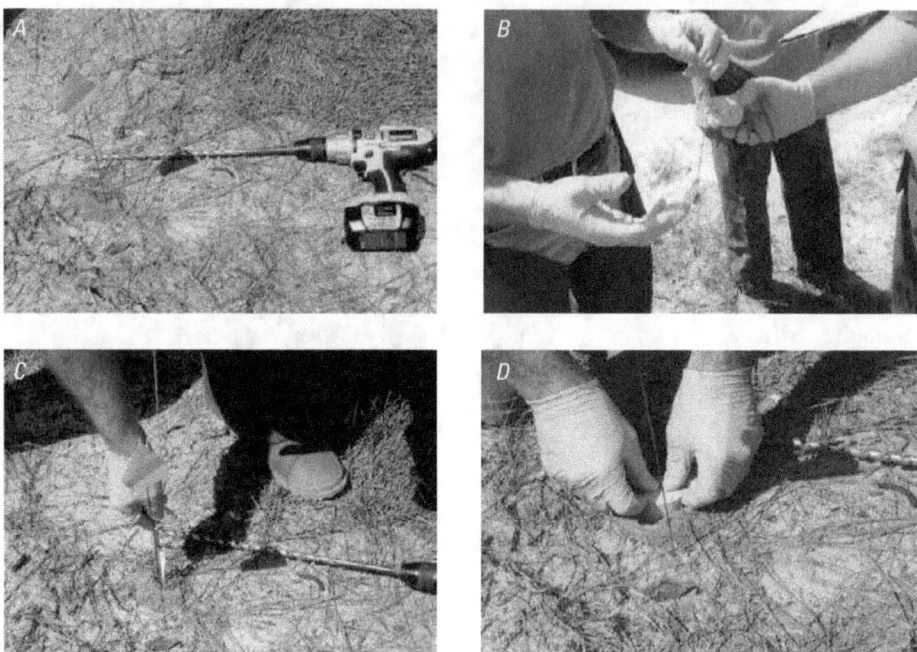

Figure 6. Installation of a passive soil-gas sampler in the landfill soil consisted of (*A*) drilling a borehole in the soil with a stainless-steel drill bit attached to a cordless drill, (*B*) attaching one end of a string to the soil-gas sampler and the other end to a cork plug, (*C*) inserting the soil-gas sampler into the borehole, and (D) sealing the borehole with the cork plug to keep out surface material and water.

compounds) as BTEX; undecane, tridecane, and pentadecane (diesel-range alkanes) as C_{11}, C_{13}, and C_{15}; 1,2,4- and 1,3,5-trimethylbenzene; *trans*- and *cis*-1,2-dichloroethene; and naphthalene and 2-methyl naphthalene. The laboratory provided method detection levels (MDL) for each of the 31 organic compounds, but did not provide MDLs for the five combined values. The reported combined value should be considered estimated (E) if the measured value of any of the individual compounds were reported as below detection level. A value of 0.00 (reporting format of W.L. Gore & Associates, Inc.) is reported for combined mass or concentration if the individual compounds included in the combined value were not detected above method detection levels and at least one of the individual compounds was reported as below detection level.

Total petroleum hydrocarbon (TPH) was one of the 31 organic analytes reported by the laboratory and was a laboratory-derived estimate based on the area under the chromatogram for all aliphatic hydrocarbons, including all gasoline-range (carbon atoms labeled C_4 to C_{10}) and diesel-range (carbon atoms labeled C_{10} to C_{20}) compounds. The laboratory provided MDLs for the hyporheic-zone (1.39 µg/L) and soil-gas (0.02 µg) TPH detections.

Samplers for the July 2010 soil-gas survey were deployed in an effort to obtain samples from all areas of the landfill study area adjacent to the unnamed tributary and were analyzed for petroleum and halogenated compounds that are not classified as explosives or chemical agents. Three unused samplers were shipped to the laboratory as trip blanks.

The results of the July 2010 soil-gas survey were used to select five sites at the former hospital landfill for a second soil-gas survey to evaluate the presence of organic compounds classified as chemical agents and explosives. The environmental samplers and trip blanks for this soil-gas survey (September 16–22, 2010) were analyzed for 11 chemical agents and 9 explosives. The five sample sites chosen for the second survey included three sites with TPH detections greater than 15.0 µg and two site with minimal detections of TPH (less than 1.2 µg) in the July 2010 soil-gas survey. These specific sample sites were chosen to evaluate the occurrence of chemical agents and explosives, if present, relative to the presence or absence of other organic constituents detected at the landfill.

Soil Samples

Composite soil samples were analyzed for inorganic constituents. The soil samples were collected at the same five locations as in the September 16–22, 2010, soil-gas survey for explosives and chemical agents. A stainless-steel hand auger was used to collect the soil samples between land surface and a depth of 6 in. (fig. 7). Organic plant material was removed from the sample in the field, if possible. The auger was washed

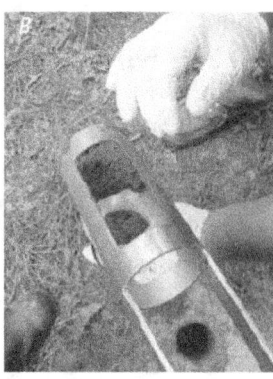

with a soap solution, rinsed with deionized water, and wiped with a paper towel prior to the collection of each sample.

Soil samples were analyzed by using Inductively Coupled Plasma-Mass Spectrometry (ICP-MS; LaDonna Choate, Research Chemist, U.S. Geological Survey, Denver, Colorado, written commun., 2009). The samples were ground into powder in the laboratory and processed by a multi-acid digestion technique prior to analysis (Crock and others, 1983). The multi-acid digestion technique combined with ICP-MS is suited for the analysis of inorganics in rocks, soils, and sediments (Briggs and Meier, 2002). Each sample was analyzed for 35 inorganic constituents, including 6 of the 8 RCRA metals (selenium and mercury were not included in the laboratory analysis). All results are rounded.

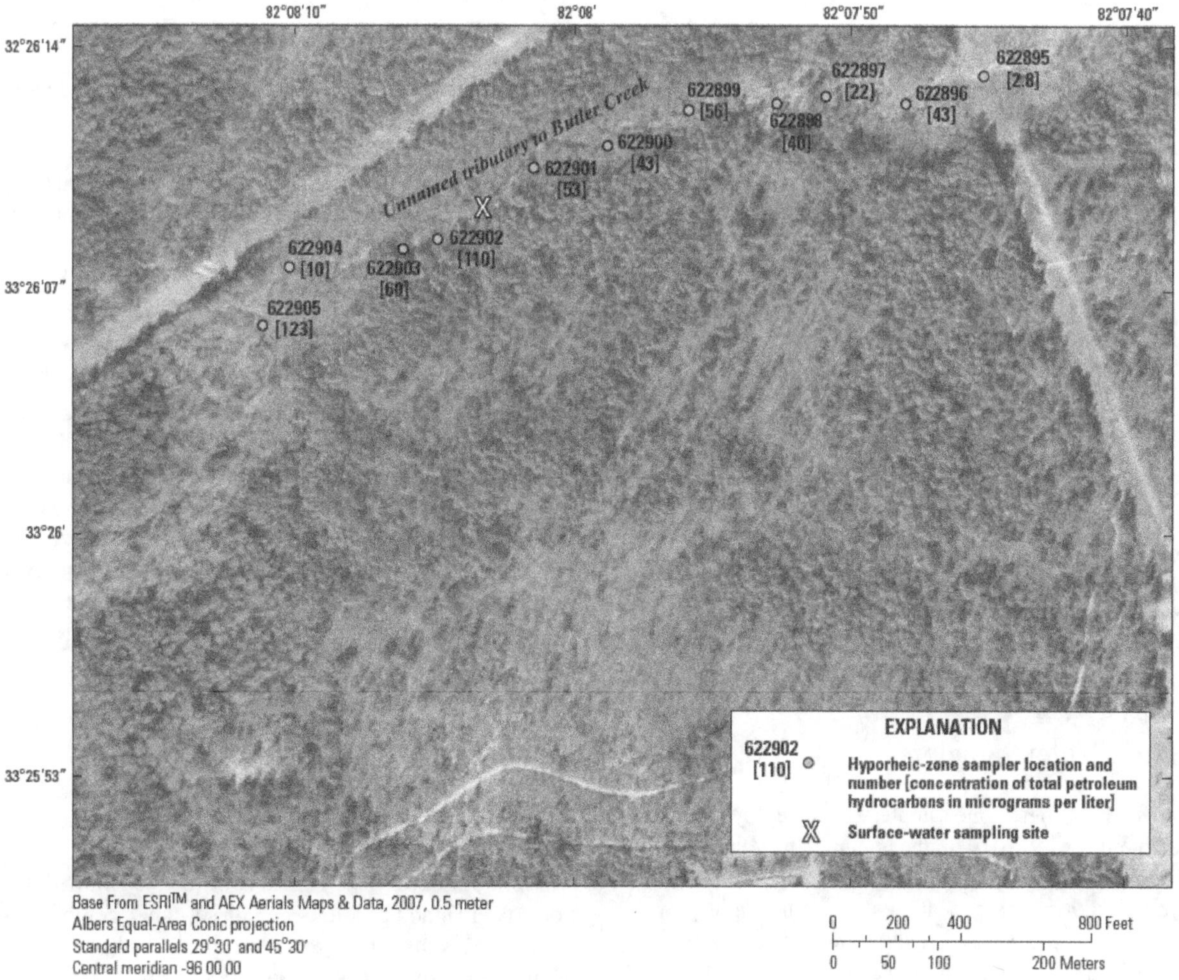

Figure 7. Soil sample (*A*) collected in the interval from land surface to a depth of 6 inches with a stainless-steel hand auger and (*B*) transferred from the auger to a plastic container for shipment to the laboratory.

Figure 8. Locations and identification numbers of hyporheic-zone samplers along the unnamed tributary to Butler Creek, and total petroleum hydrocarbon concentrations in micrograms per liter for each sampler (number in brackets), April 9, 2010, and location of the surface-water sampling site, September 8, 2010, former hospital landfill, Fort Gordon, Georgia. Method detection level for hyporheic-zone samplers is 1.39 micrograms per liter.

Surface-Water Samples

A surface-water sample was collected from the unnamed tributary of Butler Creek near the utility right-of-way at the eastern boundary of the study area under base-flow conditions on September 8, 2010. A calibrated field meter was used to monitor, measure, and record temperature, specific conductance, dissolved oxygen, and pH at each site prior to sampling (U.S. Geological Survey, variously dated). After stabilization of field parameters, bottles were submerged in the creek and filled with unfiltered water for analyses of inorganic constituents, VOCs, and SVOCs. Samples for inorganic constituents and VOCs were preserved with nitric and hydrochloric acids, respectively. SVOC samples did not require chemical preservation. All samples were immediately placed on ice and shipped overnight to the U.S. Geological Survey National Water Quality Laboratory (NWQL) in Denver, Colorado, for analysis.

The water sample was processed for 22 inorganic constituents, 85 VOCs, and 56 SVOCs (Fishman, 1993; Connor and others, 1998; Garbarino and Struzeski, 1998). Surrogates for VOCs and SVOCs were used to test analytical method recovery for laboratory blanks and set spikes. A VOC trip blank was taken to the field during sample collection and shipped to the laboratory with the environmental sample for analysis. All results are reported to a minimum reporting level provided by the laboratory and are rounded.

Results

All samples collected from the former hospital landfill study area and adjacent segment of the unnamed tributary to Butler Creek were collected from April to September 2010. The results are discussed for the hyporheic-zone survey in the unnamed tributary to Butler Creek, the passive soil-gas surveys and soil samples collected in the landfill, and surface water collected in the unnamed tributary to Butler Creek. The results of trip and method blanks for all soil-gas samplers and a VOC trip blank for the surface-water sample also are discussed to qualify environmental results for the study area.

Hyporheic-Zone Samplers

Eleven hyporheic-zone samplers were deployed and recovered on April 9, 2010, in the unnamed tributary to Butler Creek adjacent to the study area (fig. 8). Sampler 622895 was deployed at a downstream location at the utility right of way. The downstream site was selected on the basis of discussions with Fort Gordon personnel during an earlier site visit in 2009. The decision to stop at upstream sampler 622905 was based, in part, on the presence of debris in the southwestern corner of the study area (fig. 1). The 11 hyporheic-zone samplers were deployed in the creek bed near to the southern side of the creek channel and were in contact with water inside the drive

point; therefore, the results for the hyporheic-zone samplers are reported in micrograms per liter.

The hyporheic-zone results indicated that TPH and octane were the most frequently detected contaminants in groundwater beneath the creek bed (table 1). The TPH concentrations exceeded the MDL of 1.39 µg/L at all 11 sampler locations (fig. 8). The lowest TPH concentration was 2.84 µg/L in the downstream-most sampler (622895) and was the only compound to exceed its MDL in this sampler. Octane concentrations, a gasoline-range compound, exceeded the MDL of 1.39 µg/L at six of the sampler locations. The two highest TPH and octane concentrations were detected in samplers 622902 and 622905 in the upstream part of the hyporheic-zone study area. The only other specific detections of organic compounds were toluene in sampler 622902 and benzene in sampler 622904, both in the upstream part of the study area (fig. 8; table 1). None of the organic compounds requested for laboratory analysis exceeded MDLs in the trip and method blanks; therefore, the hyporheic-zone detections were accepted as environmental results.

Because TPH and octane concentrations and the only detections of benzene and toluene were detected in the upstream (western) part of the hyporheic-zone study area, the effort to delineate landfill activity in the study area was focused on the western part of the 75-acre study area outlined in figure 1. The delineation of the landfill and its environmental effects covered the part of the study area south of hyporheic-zone samplers 622902 to 622905 from the unnamed tributary to the upslope unpaved access road (fig. 1).

Soil-Gas Samplers: July 26–30, 2010

The effort to delineate landfill activity in the study area focused on the western 14 acres of the 75-acre study area because this is the part of the study area with the highest concentrations of organic compounds for the hyporheic-zone study and the part of the study area with a recognizable debris field (figs. 1, 8). The southern part of the 14-acre study area includes a debris field, and is steeper and not as heavily wooded as the central and northern parts. The approximate debris field location was in the area of samplers 637733 through 637740 (figs. 1, 9).

A total of 52 samplers were deployed for the July 26–30, 2010, soil-gas survey in the western part of the study area (fig. 9). The target compounds for this soil-gas survey were petroleum and halogenated compounds not classified as chemical agents and explosives.

The July 2010 soil-gas survey mostly identified detections of TPH, and gasoline- and diesel-range compounds (table 2). Results for the three trip blanks and two method blanks were reported as nondetections or below detection level, with the exception of two solvents. Trichloroethene (TCE) and perchloroethene (PCE) were detected in one of the trip blanks. All reported PCE detections below the trip blank mass of 0.08 µg were censored. Trichloroethene was not detected in any of the environmental samples; therefore, censoring was not required. Except for perchloroethene, all results for environmental samplers did not require censoring and are presented in table 2 and discussed in this report as environmental results.

Total petroleum hydrocarbon was detected at a soil-gas mass of 1.0 µg or greater in 28 of the 52 soil-gas samplers (fig. 9; table 2). Nine samplers had TPH soil-gas mass than exceeded 10.0 µg. The highest detection of TPH was

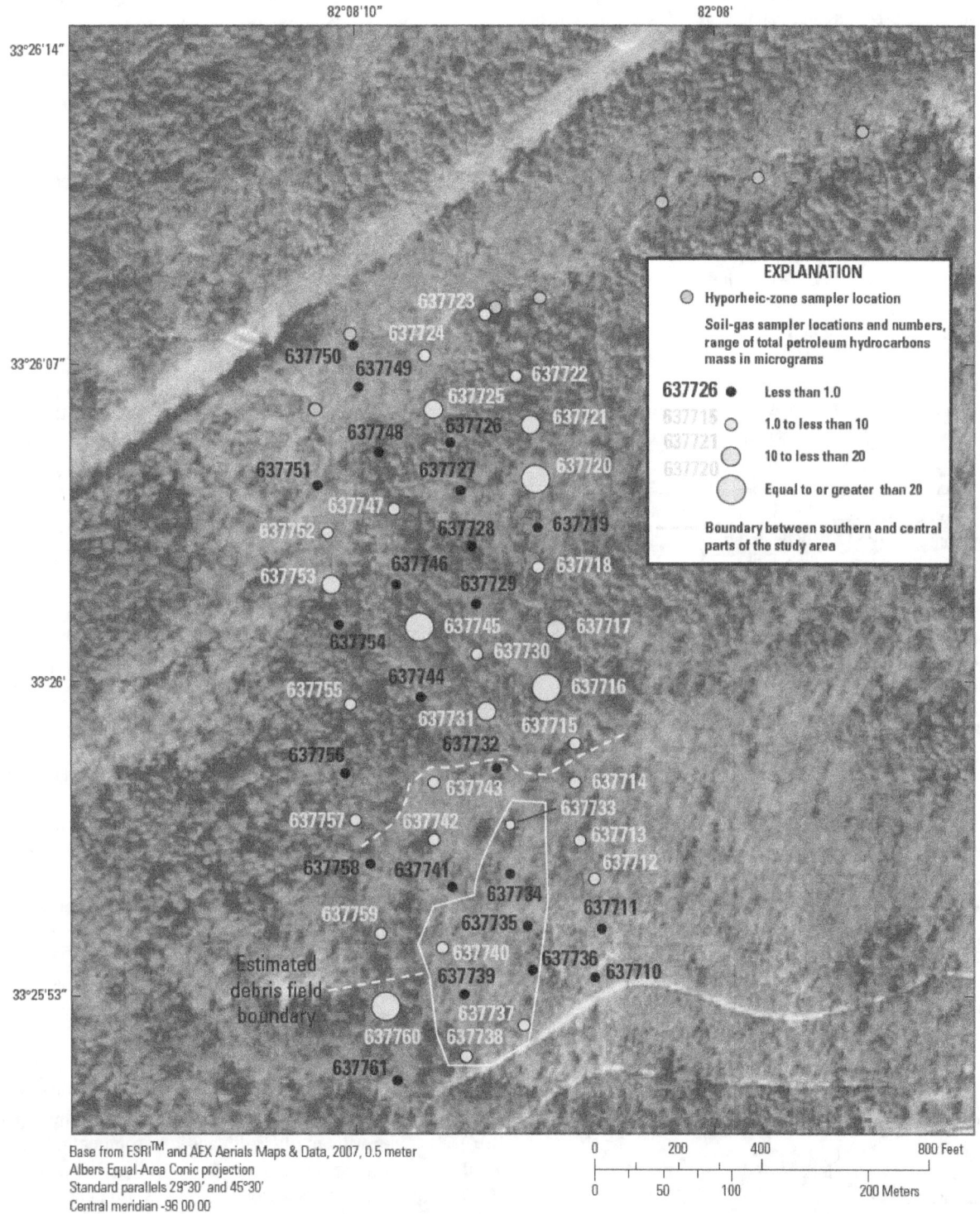

Figure 9. Locations and identification numbers of passive soil-gas samplers, and ranges of soil-gas mass for total petroleum hydrocarbons in micrograms, former hospital landfill, Fort Gordon, Georgia, July 26–30, 2010. Method detection level is 0.02 microgram.

31.72 µg in sampler 637760 near the debris field in the southern part of the soil-gas study area. The other eight samplers with TPH mass greater than 10.0 µg were downslope from the debris field in the central and northern parts of the 14-acre soil-gas study area. This part of the study area is more heavily wooded and has more underbrush than the southern part near the debris field and is boggy in a few spots, indicating a shallow groundwater table.

Detections of BTEX were reported as a combined mass for benzene, toluene, ethylbenzene and *ortho*-xylene with MDLs of 0.02 µg, and *meta*- and *para*-xylene with an MDL of 0.03 µg, but xylene and ethylbenzene were not detected in any of the samplers (table 2). Therefore, all BTEX results are censored at 0.02 µg in figure 10 and are presented as environmental results. Five samplers had BTEX detections as soil-gas mass of 0.02 µg or greater (fig. 10). All detections were downslope from the debris field in the central and northern parts of the soil-gas study area.

Diesel was reported by the laboratory as a combined mass for undecane with an MDL of 0.04 µg, and tridecane and pentadecane with MDLs of 0.02 µg (table 2). Each of the three diesel compounds was detected in at least one of the samplers; therefore, results for the combined diesel mass were censored at the higher MDL of 0.04 µg in figure 11 for discussion as environmental results in this report. Nine detections of soil-gas mass as diesel exceeded 0.04 µg (fig. 11; table 2). The highest soil-gas mass for diesel was detected in the same sampler (637760) that had the highest soil-gas mass for TPH in the southern part of the study area. The other eight detections of diesel were downslope from the debris field (north and west) in the central and northern parts of the soil-gas study area.

The remaining compounds reported for environmental samplers as mass and combined mass in table 2 were reported as nondetections, below detection levels, or 0.00 µg, except for PCE. PCE was detected in four samplers at a soil-gas mass greater than the MDL (0.02 µg), but also was detected in one of the trip blanks. Sampler 637757 had a PCE soil-gas mass of 0.21 µg, which was the only sampler out with PCE mass that exceeded the PCE mass in the trip blank. Because of the detectable PCE mass in the trip blank, the PCE reported in sampler 637757 is the only detection that can be considered as an environmental result. This detection occurred in the central part of the soil-gas study area to the west and downslope of the debris field. TCE was detected at a soil-gas mass of 0.03 µg (MDL = 0.02 µg) in the same trip blank (sampler 637772) as the PCE, but was not detected in any of the deployed environmental samplers.

Soil-Gas Samplers: September 16–22, 2010

Five soil-gas samplers were deployed on September 16 and recovered on September 22, 2010 (fig. 12). These samplers were analyzed for VOCs and SVOCs classified as chemical agents or explosives and were deployed at the same locations as five of the July 2010 soil-gas samplers (table 3). None of the chemical agents or explosives exceeded

an MDL in deployed soil-gas samplers, except for a detection of chloroacetophenone in sampler 644234 at a soil-gas mass of 0.13 µg (table 3). The chloroacetophenone was detected at the same soil-gas location as the highest TPH detection in the southern part of the soil-gas study area. One of the uses of chloroacetophenone during the active period of waste disposal at the landfill (1960s and 1970s) was as a component of tear gas (also known as mace).

Three additional chemical warfare agents were reported in environmental samplers as below detection levels—benzothiazole, *para*-chlorophenyl methyl sulfide, and *para*-chlorophenyl methyl sulfone (table 3). Soil-gas mass for *para*-chlorophenyl methyl sulfone was reported as below detection level in the method blanks and all five trip blanks, indicating a systemic contamination problem for this compound; therefore, the results are not accepted as environmental results. Soil-gas mass for *para*-chlorophenyl methyl sulfide was reported as below detection level in one method blank; therefore, the result for sample 644232 is not accepted as an environmental result. Soil-gas masses as benzothiazole were reported as non detections in all trip and method blanks, so the masses of this compound reported as below detection level in three environmental samplers can be accepted as environmental results with an uncertain mass. All laboratory results for the nine explosive compounds were reported as non detections in environmental samplers.

Soil Samples

Composite soil samples were collected at five locations (fig. 12). Three sampling locations had detections of TPH soil-gas mass of greater than 18 µg in the July 2010 soil-gas samplers. Soil samples 2 and 4 were collected at the same locations as the July 2010 soil-gas samplers 637736 and 637718, respectively, which had detections of TPH soil-gas mass of 0.67 and 1.19 µg. Therefore, the locations of soil samples 2 and 4 were considered relatively clean of VOC and SVOCs, compared to the other three locations. Quality-control samples were not collected for soil samples.

The soil samples were analyzed for 35 inorganic constituents, including 6 of the 8 RCRA metals (selenium and mercury were excluded; table 4). Concentrations were compared to the USEPA Regional Screening Levels (RSLs) for Industrial Soils (U.S. Environmental Protection Agency, 2009a). Concentrations for 19 of the 35 constituents also were compared to ambient, uncontaminated (background) levels for soils across the adjacent State of South Carolina (South Carolina Department of Health and Environmental Control, 2002) because no similar background values were available for Georgia. The comparison remained valid because Georgia and South Carolina have similar geologic and land-use histories.

At all five locations, constituent concentrations in soil samples did not exceed the USEPA RSLs (table 4). Inorganic

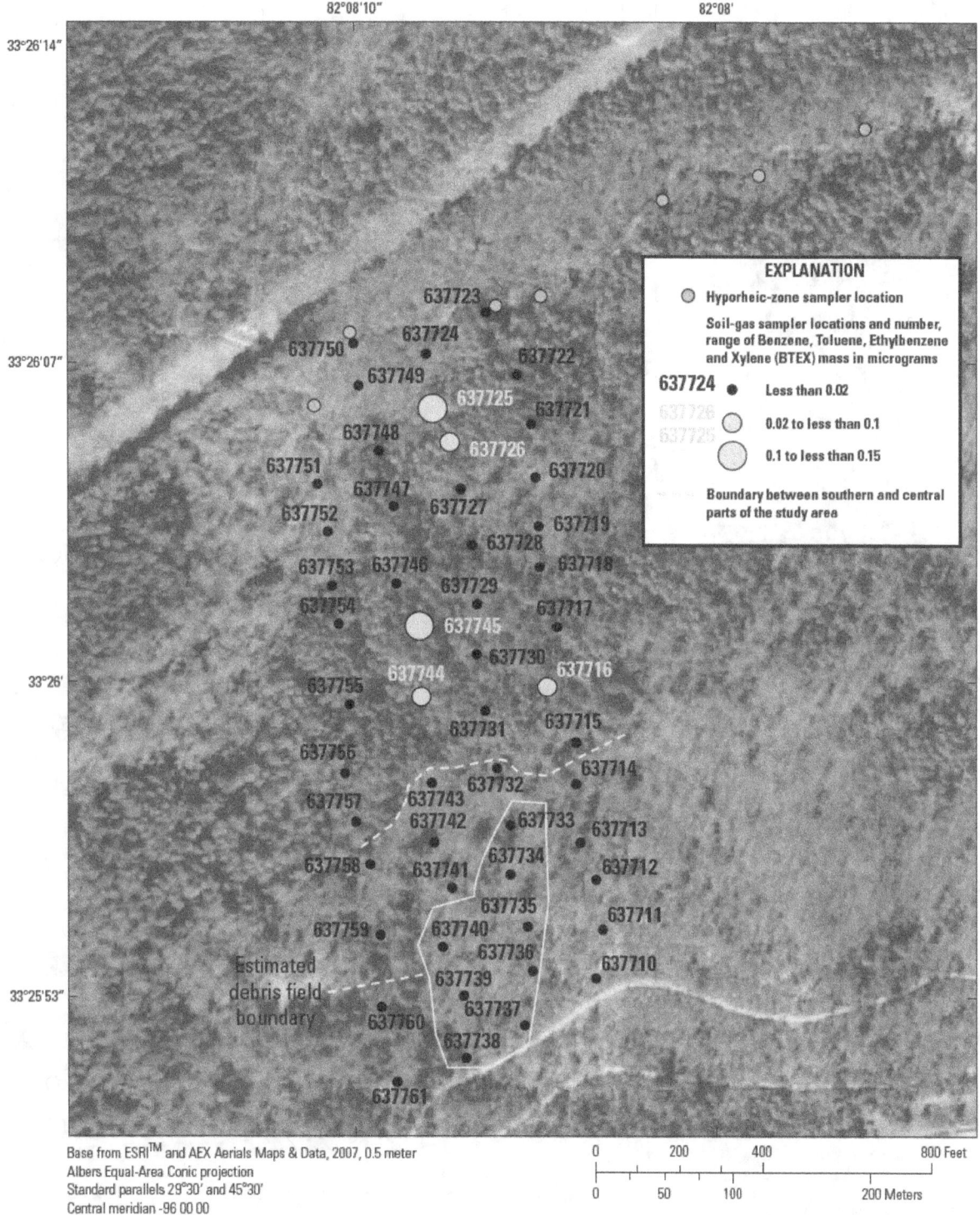

Figure 10. Locations and identification numbers of passive soil-gas samplers, and ranges of combined soil-gas mass for benzene, toluene, ethylbenzene, and xylene (BTEX gasoline compounds) in micrograms, former hospital landfill, Fort Gordon, Georgia, July 26–30, 2010. Method detection levels for the benzene and toluene compounds (ethylbenzene and xylene not detected) equal 0.02 micrograms. All combined masses, therefore, are censored at less than 0.02 microgram.

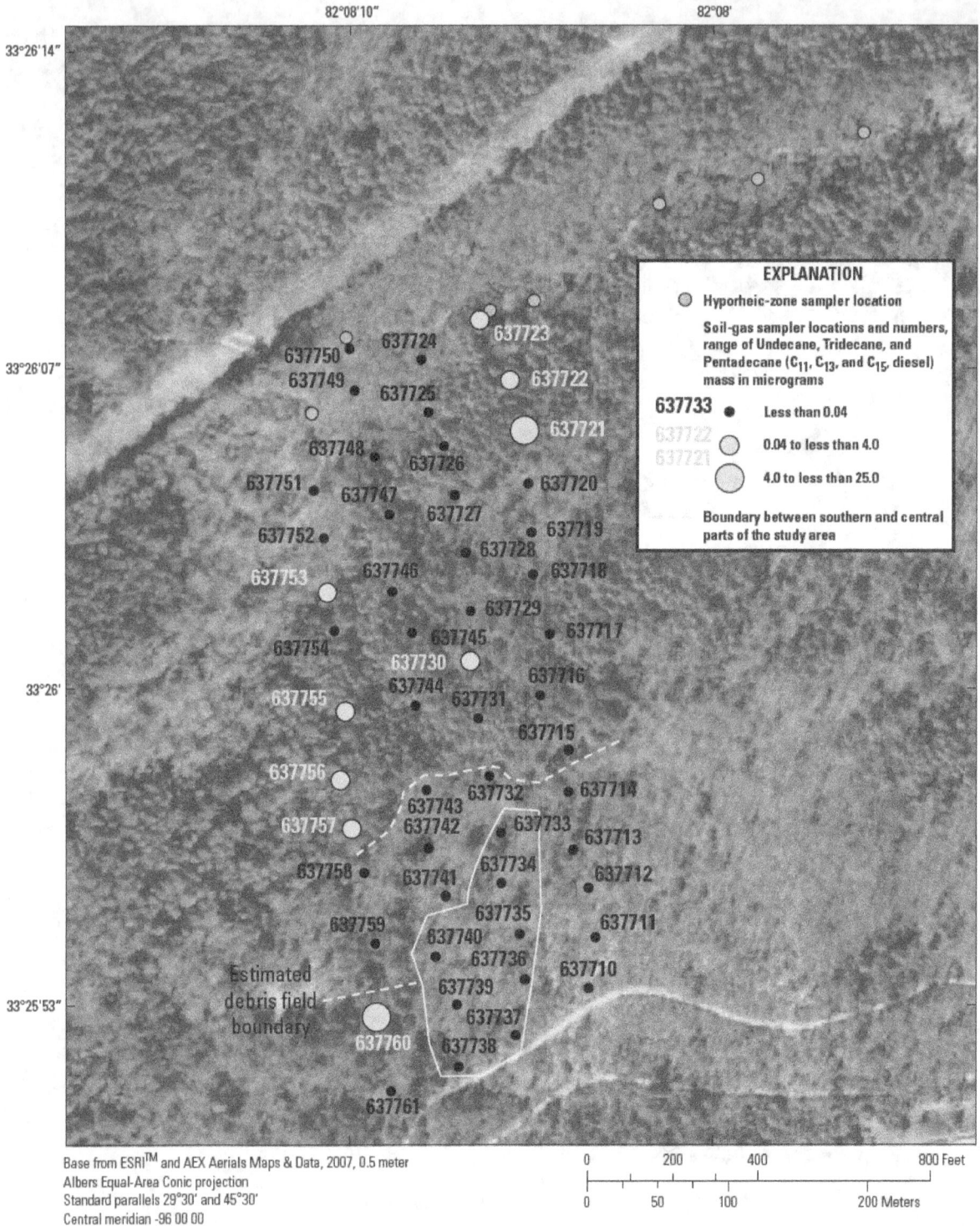

Figure 11. Locations and identification numbers of passive soil-gas samplers, and ranges of combined soil-gas mass for undecane, tridecane, and pentadecane (C_{11}, C_{13}, and C_{15}, diesel compounds) in micrograms, former hospital landfill, Fort Gordon, Georgia, July 26–30, 2010. Method detection levels for the three diesel compounds range from 0.02 to 0.04 microgram. All combined masses, therefore, are censored at less than 0.04 microgram.

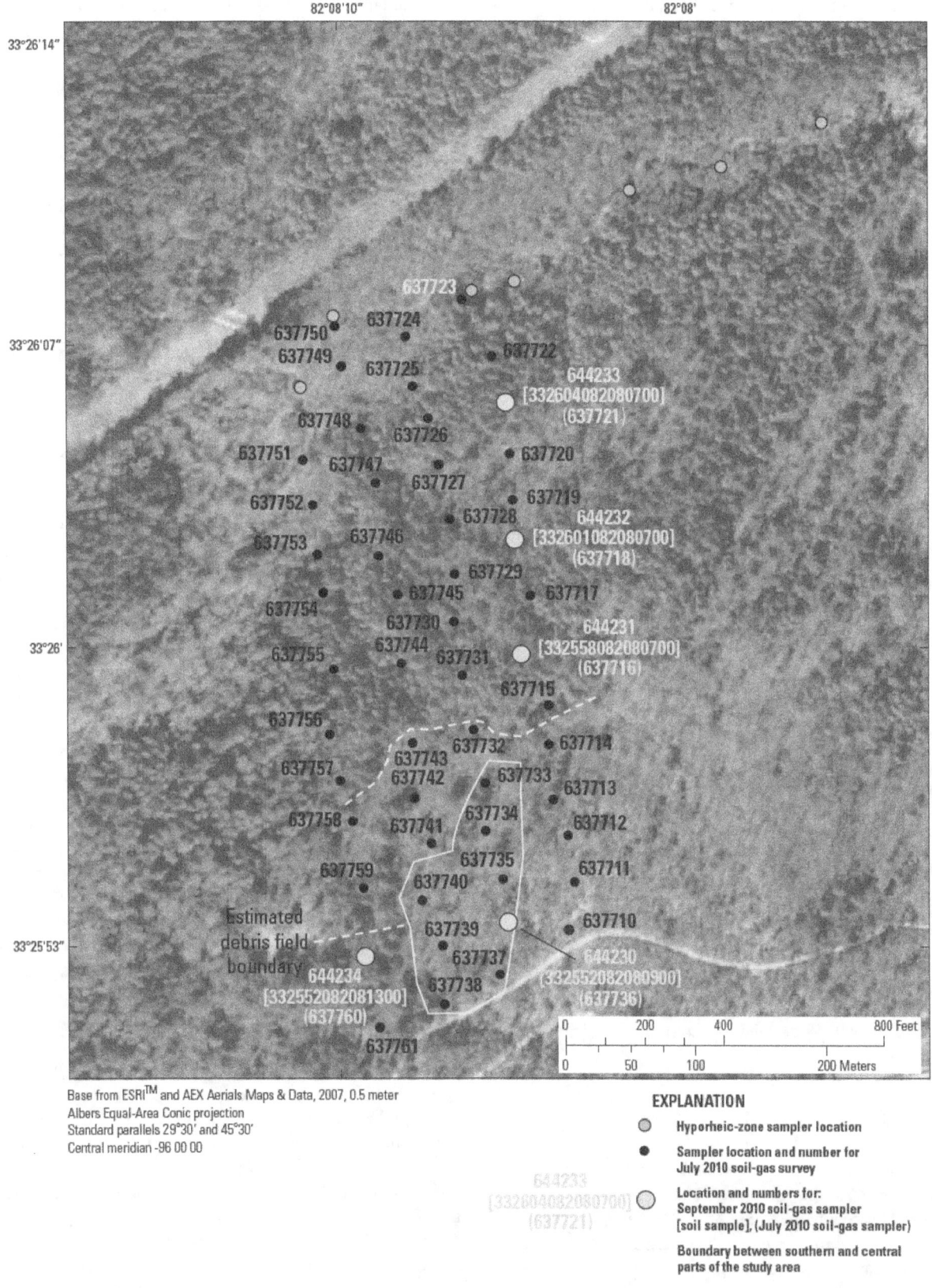

Figure 12. Locations and identification numbers of September 2010 soil-gas samplers analyzed for volatile and semivolatile organic compounds classified as chemical warfare agents and explosives, August 30, 2010, and soil samples analyzed for inorganic constituents, former hospital landfill study area, Fort Gordon, Georgia.

concentrations were, however, higher than background conditions reported in South Carolina for barium at all five sample locations, aluminum at three sample locations, and potassium at two locations. Inorganic concentrations were close to, yet still higher, than background concentrations for chromium in sample 1, and for lead and zinc in sample 2 in the southern part of the soil-gas study area. Similarly, sodium concentrations in sample 4 were slightly above background levels in the central part of the study area.

Surface-Water Samples

One surface-water sample was collected from the unnamed tributary on September 8, 2010, and was shipped with a VOC trip blank to the NWQL. The sample was collected between hyporheic-zone samplers 622901 and 622902 to focus on surface-water quality in the western end of the hyporheic-zone study area (fig. 8; table 5).

A concentration for an inorganic constituent or an organic compound was reported as a quantitative detection if it was greater than the laboratory reporting level (Childress and others, 1999). A concentration was reported as a semiquantitative estimate (E) in table 5 if the value was between the laboratory reporting level and the NWQL long-term MDL for the constituent. The percentage recovery for all surrogates was satisfactory, with the exception of the SVOC surrogate for phenol, which could result in an underestimation of concentrations for phenol and SVOCs with similar properties.

All results for the VOC trip blank were reported as less than the laboratory reporting level, except for toluene (table 5). The toluene concentration in the surface-water sample, however, did not exceed the laboratory reporting level of 0.018 µg/L.

The iron concentrations of 1,340 µg/L and the aluminum concentrations of 58.5 µg/L exceeded Federal secondary drinking-water standards of 300 and 50 µg/L, respectively (U.S. Environmental Protection Agency, 2009b). The VOCs detected in the surface-water sample were chloroform with an estimated concentration of 0.0196 µg/L and trichlorofluoromethane with a concentration of 0.086 µg/L (table 5). Estimated concentrations of two SVOCs also were detected—fluoranthene at 0.013 µg/L and isophorone at 0.015 µg/L.

Summary

The U.S. Geological Survey, in cooperation with the U.S. Department of the Army Environmental and Natural Resources Management Office of the U.S. Army Signal Center and Fort Gordon, Georgia, assessed soil gas, soil, and water for contaminants at the former hospital landfill and the adjacent segment of an unnamed tributary to Butler Creek from April to September 2010. Part of the cantonment area consists of an abandoned landfill near the Dwight D. Eisenhower Army Medical Center, known as the former

hospital landfill (the landfill). The study area for the investigation is located in the northern part of the cantonment area and included 75 acres between an unnamed tributary to Butler Creek and an unpaved access road south of the tributary. The site assessment consisted of (a) a preliminary survey along the unnamed tributary to Butler Creek to identify potential areas of volatile and semivolatile organic compounds in the hyporheic zone adjacent to the landfill, (b) two soil-gas surveys for organic compounds and soil samples for inorganic constituents in the landfill, and (c) collection of surface water for organic compounds and inorganic constituents from the adjacent segment of the unnamed tributary.

Eleven hyporheic-zone samplers were deployed and recovered on February 12, 2010, in the unnamed tributary to Butler Creek adjacent to the study area. Total petroleum hydrocarbons (TPH) detected in all 11 samplers and octane (a gasoline compound) detected in six samplers were the most frequently detected contaminants in groundwater beneath the creek bed. The two highest TPH and octane concentrations were detected in samplers 622902 and 622905 in the upstream part of the hyporheic-zone study area. Other gasoline compounds detected included toluene in sampler 622902 and benzene in sampler 622904, both in the upstream part of the study area.

The effort to delineate landfill activity in the study area focused on the western 14 acres of the 75-acre study area where the hyporheic-zone study identified the highest concentrations of organic compounds. A debris field also was identified in the southern part of the western 14 acres. The southern part of this 14-acre study area, including the debris field, is steeper and not as heavily wooded as the central and northern parts.

The 52 samplers used for the July 2010 soil-gas survey in the western-most 14 acres of the 75-acre study area were deployed on July 26, 2010, and recovered on July 30, 2010, for the detection of petroleum and halogenated compounds not classified as chemical agents and explosives. The survey mostly identified detections of TPH, and gasoline and diesel compounds. The highest detection of TPH was 31.72 micrograms in sampler 637760 near the debris field in the southern part of the soil-gas study area. Another eight samplers with TPH mass greater than 10.0 micrograms were downslope from the debris field in the central and northern parts of the soil-gas study area. The combined soil-gas mass for benzene, toluene, ethylbenzene, and xylene was 0.02 microgram or greater in five samplers; all detections were downslope from the debris field in the central and northern parts of the soil-gas study area. The highest soil-gas mass for diesel was detected in the same sampler (637760) that had the highest soil-gas mass for TPH in the southern part of the study area. Eight diesel detections also were downslope from the debris field (north and west) in the central and northern parts of the soil-gas study area. Perchloroethene was detected in four samplers at a soil-gas mass greater than the method detection level of 0.02 microgram, but also was detected in one of the trip blanks. Sampler 637757 in the southwestern part of the soil-gas study area had a perchloroethene soil-gas mass of 0.21 microgram, which was the only sampler that exceeded the soil-gas mass in the trip blank.

Five soil-gas samplers were deployed on September 16 and recovered on September 22, 2010, and were analyzed for organic compounds classified as chemical agents or explosives. Chloroacetophenone (a tear gas component) was detected at the same soil-gas location as the highest TPH detection in the southern part of the soil-gas study area. This was the only detection of a chemical agent or explosive that exceeded its method detection level (0.10 microgram).

Composite soil samples were collected at five locations and were analyzed for 35 inorganic constituents. At all five locations, constituent concentrations did not exceed USEPA regional screening levels.

One surface-water sample was collected from the unnamed tributary on September 8, 2010, between hyporheic-zone samplers 622901 and 622902 to focus on surface-water quality in the western end of the hyporheic-zone study area. Secondary drinking water standards were exceeded for aluminum and iron. The only organic detections in the surface-water sample were a detection of trichlorofluoromethane and estimated concentrations of chloroform, fluoranthene, and isophorone.

References Cited

American Society for Testing and Materials, 2006, Standard guide for soil gas monitoring in the vadose zone: West Conshohocken, PA, ASTM D5314-92, 36 p.

Briggs, P.H., and Meier, A.L., 2002, The determination of forty-two elements in geological materials by inductively coupled plasma-mass spectrometry, *in* Taggart, J.E., Jr., ed., Analytical methods for chemical analysis of geologic and other materials, U.S. Geological Survey: U.S. Geological Survey Open-File Report 02–223, chapter I, 20 p.

Childress, C.J.O., Foreman, W.T., Connor, B.F., and Maloney, T.J., 1999, New reporting procedures based on long-term method detection levels and some considerations for interpretations of water-quality data provided by the U.S. Geological Survey National Water Quality Laboratory: U.S. Geological Survey Open File Report 99–193, 19 p.

Connor, B.F., Rose, D.L., Noriega, M.C., Murtagh, L.K., and Abney, S.A., 1998, Methods of analysis by the U.S. Geological Survey National Water Quality Laboratory— Determination of 86 volatile organic compounds in water by gas chromatography/mass spectrometry, including detections less than reporting limits: U.S. Geological Survey Open-File Report 97–829, 78 p.

Crock, J.G., Lichte, F.L., and Briggs, P.H., 1983, Determination of elements in National Bureau of Standards geological materials SRM 278 obsidian and SRM 688 basalt by inductively coupled plasma-atomic emission spectroscopy: Geostandards Newsletter, v. 7, no. 2, p. 335–340.

Fishman, M.J., ed., 1993, Methods of analysis by the U.S. Geological Survey National Water Quality Laboratory—Determination of inorganic and organic constituents in water and fluvial sediments: U.S. Geological Survey Open-File Report 93–125, 217 p.

Garbarino, J.R., and Struzeski, T.M., 1998, Methods of analysis by the U.S. Geological Survey National Water Quality Laboratory–Determination of elements in whole-water digests using inductively coupled plasma-optical emission spectrometry and inductively coupled plasma-mass spectrometry: U.S. Geological Survey Open-File Report 98–165, 101 p.

Gregory, M.B., Stamey, T.C., and Wellborn, J.B., 2001, Ecological characterization of streams, and fish-tissue analysis for mercury and lead at selected locations, Fort Gordon, Georgia, June 1999 to May 2000: U.S. Geological Survey Open-File Report 01–203, 14 p.

Hetrick, J.H., 1992, A geologic atlas of the Wrens-Augusta area: Georgia Geologic Survey Geologic Atlas no. 8, 2 plates.

International Organization for Standardization, 1990, ISO guide 25—General requirements for the competence of calibration and testing laboratories (3d ed.): New York, American National Standards Institute.

South Carolina Department of Health and Environmental Control, 2002, Environmental Surveillance and Oversight Program data report, 2002, accessed February 11, 2010, at *http://www.scdhec.gov/environment/envserv/docs/esop_datarpt_02.pdf.*

U.S. Environmental Protection Agency, 1998, Environmental technology verification report soil gas sampling technology: EPA/600/R–98/095, accessed May 11, 2011, at *http://www.epa.gov/nrmrl/lrpcd/site/reports/600r98095/600r98095.htm.*

U.S. Environmental Protection Agency, 2006, The method of evaluating solid waste—Physical chemical methods (3d ed.), final update IV of SW–846, accessed March 22, 2010, at *http://www.epa.gov/fedrgstr/EPA-WASTE/2008/January/Day-03/f25575.htm.*

U.S. Environmental Protection Agency, 2009a, Regional screening level tables, accessed January 12, 2010, at *http://www.epa.gov/reg3hwmd/risk/human/rb-concentration_table/Generic_Tables/index.htm.*

U.S. Environmental Protection Agency, 2009b, Regional screening level tables, accessed January 23, 2010, at *http://www.epa.gov/reg3hwmd/risk/human/rb-concentration_table/Generic_Tables/index.htm.*

U.S. Geological Survey, variously dated, National field manual for the collection of water-quality data: U.S. Geological Survey Techniques of Water-Resource Investigation, book 9, chaps. A1–A9, accessed May 11, 2011, at *http://water.usgs.gov/owq/FieldManual/.*

Williams, L.J., 2007, Hydrogeology and potentiometric surface of the Dublin and Midville aquifer systems in Richmond County, Georgia, January 2007: U.S. Geological Survey Scientific Investigations Map 2982, 1 sheet.

W.L. Gore & Associates, Inc., 2004, GORETM surveys for site assessment & monitoring, accessed February 24, 2011, at *http://www.gore.com/MungoBlobs/239/659/surveys_environmental_brochure.pdf.*

Table 1   17

Table 1. Concentrations of volatile and semivolatile organic compounds detected in the passive soil-gas samplers deployed and collected in the water-saturated hyporheic zone of an unnamed tributary of Butler Creek adjacent to the former hospital landfill, Fort Gordon, Georgia, April 9, 2010.

[Unrounded data provided by W.L. Gore & Associates, Inc.; MDL, method detection level; N/A, not applicable; mg/L, micrograms per liter; nd, not detected; samplers 622906 and 622907 are trip blanks; the method blank associated with this data set had no detections above the method detection level and is not included in this table]

Organic compound	MDL (μg/L)	Sampler 622895	Sampler 622896	Sampler 622897	Sampler 622898	Sampler 622899	Sampler 622900	Sampler 622901
Total petroleum hydrocarbons (TPH)	1.39	2.84	42.58	22.14	40.39	56.23	42.92	52.59
BTEX (gasoline)[1]	N/A	0.00	nd	nd	nd	nd	nd	nd
Benzene	1.39	bdl	nd	nd	nd	nd	nd	nd
Toluene	1.39	nd	nd	nd	nd	nd	nd	nd
Ethylbenzene	1.39	nd	nd	nd	nd	nd	nd	nd
meta-, *para*-, Xylene	2.08	nd	nd	nd	nd	nd	nd	nd
ortho-Xylene	1.39	nd	nd	nd	nd	nd	nd	nd
C_{11}, C_{13}, and C_{15} (diesel)[1]	N/A	nd	nd	nd	nd	nd	nd	nd
Undecane	2.77	nd	nd	nd	nd	nd	nd	nd
Tridecane	1.39	nd	nd	nd	nd	nd	nd	nd
Pentadecane	1.39	nd	nd	nd	nd	nd	nd	nd
Octane	1.39	nd	1.43	bdl	bdl	1.74	bdl	1.53
Methyl *tert*-butyl ether	4.16	nd	nd	nd	nd	nd	nd	nd
Trimethylbenzene[1]	N/A	nd	nd	nd	nd	nd	nd	nd
1,2,4-Trimethylbenzene	1.39	nd	nd	nd	nd	nd	nd	nd
1,3,5-Trimethylbenzene	2.08	nd	nd	nd	nd	nd	nd	nd
1,2-Dichlorobenzene	1.39	nd	nd	nd	nd	nd	nd	nd
1,3-Dichlorobenzene	1.39	nd	nd	nd	nd	nd	nd	nd
1,4-Dichlorobenzene	1.39	nd	nd	nd	nd	nd	nd	nd
Chlorobenzene	1.39	nd	nd	nd	nd	nd	nd	nd
Chloroform	1.39	nd	nd	nd	nd	nd	nd	nd
cis- and *trans*-1,2-Dichloroethene[1]	N/A	nd	nd	nd	nd	nd	nd	nd
trans-1,2-Dichloroethene	3.19	nd	nd	nd	nd	nd	nd	nd
cis-1,2-Dichloroethene	2.14	nd	nd	nd	nd	nd	nd	nd
Trichloroethene	1.39	nd	nd	nd	nd	nd	nd	nd
Tetrachloroethene	1.39	nd	nd	nd	nd	nd	nd	nd
1,1-Dichloroethane	1.39	nd	nd	nd	nd	nd	nd	nd
1,2-Dichloroethane	1.39	nd	nd	nd	nd	nd	nd	nd
1,1,1-Trichloroethane	2.08	nd	nd	nd	nd	nd	nd	nd
1,1,2-Trichloroethane	1.39	nd	nd	nd	nd	nd	nd	nd
1,1,1,2-Tetrachloroethane	2.08	nd	nd	nd	nd	nd	nd	nd
1,1,2,2-Tetrachloroethane	1.39	nd	nd	nd	nd	nd	nd	nd
Carbon tetrachloride	2.08	nd	nd	nd	nd	nd	nd	nd
Naphthalene and 2-Methyl napthalene[1]	N/A	nd	nd	nd	nd	nd	nd	nd
Naphthalene	1.39	nd	nd	nd	nd	nd	nd	nd
2-Methyl naphthalene	1.39	nd	nd	nd	nd	nd	nd	nd

Table 1.   Concentration of volatile and semivolatile organic compounds detected in the passive soil-gas samplers deployed and collected in the water-saturated hyporheic zone of an unnamed tributary of Butler Creek adjacent to the former hospital landfill, Fort Gordon, Georgia, April 9, 2010.—Continued

[Unrounded data provided by W.L. Gore & Associates, Inc.; MDL, method detection level; N/A, not applicable; µg/L, micrograms per liter; nd, not detected; samplers 622906 and 622907 are trip blanks; the method blank associated with this data set had no detections above the method detection level and is not included in this table]

Organic compound	MDL (µg/L)	Sampler 622902	Sampler 622903	Sampler 622904	Sampler 622905	Sampler 622906	Sampler 622907
Total petroleum hydrocarbons (TPH)	1.39	110.17	59.86	9.95	122.89	nd	nd
BTEX (gasoline)[1]	N/A	2.12	nd	3.90	nd	nd	nd
Benzene	1.39	nd	nd	3.90	nd	nd	nd
Toluene	1.39	2.12	nd	nd	nd	nd	nd
Ethylbenzene	1.39	nd	nd	nd	nd	nd	nd
meta-, *para-*, Xylene	2.08	nd	nd	nd	nd	nd	nd
*ortho-*Xylene	1.39	nd	nd	nd	nd	nd	nd
C_{11}, C_{13}, and C_{15} (diesel)[1]	N/A	nd	0.00	nd	nd	nd	nd
Undecane	2.77	nd	nd	nd	nd	nd	nd
Tridecane	1.39	nd	nd	nd	nd	nd	nd
Pentadecane	1.39	nd	bdl	nd	nd	nd	nd
Octane	1.39	3.14	1.82	nd	3.81	nd	nd
Methyl *tert*-butyl ether	4.16	nd	nd	nd	nd	nd	nd
Trimethylbenzene[1]	N/A	nd	nd	nd	nd	nd	nd
1,2,4-Trimethylbenzene	1.39	nd	nd	nd	nd	nd	nd
1,3,5-Trimethylbenzene	2.08	nd	nd	nd	nd	nd	nd
1,2-Dichlorobenzene	1.39	nd	nd	nd	nd	nd	nd
1,3-Dichlorobenzene	1.39	nd	nd	nd	nd	nd	nd
1,4-Dichlorobenzene	1.39	nd	nd	nd	nd	nd	nd
Chlorobenzene	1.39	nd	nd	nd	nd	nd	nd
Chloroform	1.39	nd	nd	nd	nd	nd	nd
cis- and *trans*-1,2-Dichloroethene[1]	N/A	nd	nd	nd	nd	nd	nd
trans-1,2-Dichloroethene	3.19	nd	nd	nd	nd	nd	nd
cis-1,2-Dichloroethene	2.14	nd	nd	nd	nd	nd	nd
Trichloroethene	1.39	nd	nd	nd	nd	nd	nd
Tetrachloroethene	1.39	nd	nd	nd	nd	nd	nd
1,1-Dichloroethane	1.39	nd	nd	nd	nd	nd	nd
1,2-Dichloroethane	1.39	nd	nd	nd	nd	nd	nd
1,1,1-Trichloroethane	2.08	nd	nd	nd	nd	nd	nd
1,1,2-Trichloroethane	1.39	nd	nd	nd	nd	nd	nd
1,1,1,2-Tetrachloroethane	2.08	nd	nd	nd	nd	nd	nd
1,1,2,2-Tetrachloroethane	1.39	nd	nd	nd	nd	nd	nd
Carbon tetrachloride	2.08	nd	nd	nd	nd	nd	nd
Naphthalene and 2-Methyl napthalene[1]	N/A	nd	nd	nd	nd	nd	nd
Naphthalene	1.39	nd	nd	nd	nd	nd	nd
2-Methyl naphthalene	1.39	nd	nd	nd	nd	nd	nd

[1] Combined concentration for two or more compounds with no method detection level provided by laboratory.

Table 2   19

Table 2. Mass of volatile and semivolatile organic compounds detected in passive soil-gas samplers deployed and recovered in the soil of the former hospital landfill, Fort Gordon, Georgia, July 26–30, 2010.

[Unrounded data provided by W.L. Gore & Associates, Inc.; MDL, method detection level; μg, micrograms; N/A, not applicable; nd, not detected; bdl, below detection level; E, the reported value for a combined mass should be considered estimated if the mass of any of the individual compounds were reported as bdl; a value of 0.00 (reporting format of W.L. Gore & Associates, Inc.) is reported for a combined mass if the individual compounds included in the combined mass were not detected above method detection levels and at least one of the individual compounds was reported as bdl; samplers 637772, 637773, and 637774 are trip blanks]

Organic compound	MDL (μg)	Sampler 637710	Sampler 637711	Sampler 637712	Sampler 637713	Sampler 637714	Sampler 637715	Sampler 637716
Total petroleum hydrocarbons (TPH)	0.02	0.84	0.98	1.60	1.27	1.93	1.68	22.84
BTEX (gasoline)[1]	N/A	nd	nd	nd	nd	nd	nd	0.06
Benzene	0.02	nd	nd	nd	nd	nd	nd	nd
Toluene	0.02	nd	nd	nd	nd	nd	nd	0.06
Ethylbenzene	0.02	nd	nd	nd	nd	nd	nd	nd
meta-, *para-*, Xylene	0.03	nd	nd	nd	nd	nd	nd	nd
ortho-Xylene	0.02	nd	nd	nd	nd	nd	nd	nd
C_{11}, C_{13}, and C_{15} (diesel)[1]	N/A	nd	nd	nd	nd	nd	nd	0.00
Undecane	0.04	nd	nd	nd	nd	nd	nd	nd
Tridecane	0.02	nd	nd	nd	nd	nd	nd	nd
Pentadecane	0.02	nd	nd	nd	nd	nd	nd	bdl
Octane	0.02	nd	nd	nd	nd	nd	nd	nd
Methyl *tert*-butyl ether	0.03	nd	nd	nd	nd	nd	nd	nd
Trimethylbenzene[1]	N/A	nd	nd	nd	nd	nd	nd	0.00
1,2,4-Trimethylbenzene	0.02	nd	nd	nd	nd	nd	nd	bdl
1,3,5-Trimethylbenzene	0.03	nd	nd	nd	nd	nd	nd	nd
1,2-Dichlorobenzene	0.02	nd	nd	nd	nd	nd	nd	nd
1,3-Dichlorobenzene	0.02	nd	nd	nd	nd	nd	nd	nd
1,4-Dichlorobenzene	0.02	nd	nd	nd	nd	nd	nd	nd
Chlorobenzene	0.02	nd	nd	nd	nd	nd	nd	nd
Chloroform	0.02	nd	nd	nd	nd	nd	nd	nd
cis- and *trans*-1,2-Dichloroethene[1]	N/A	nd	nd	nd	nd	nd	nd	nd
trans-1,2-Dichloroethene	0.04	nd	nd	nd	nd	nd	nd	nd
cis-1,2-Dichloroethene	0.03	nd	nd	nd	nd	nd	nd	nd
Trichloroethene	0.02	nd	nd	nd	nd	nd	nd	nd
Tetrachloroethene	0.02	nd	nd	nd	nd	0.04	nd	nd
1,1-Dichloroethane	0.02	nd	nd	nd	nd	nd	nd	nd
1,2-Dichloroethane	0.02	nd	nd	nd	nd	nd	nd	nd
1,1,1-Trichloroethane	0.03	nd	nd	nd	nd	nd	nd	nd
1,1,2-Trichloroethane	0.02	nd	nd	nd	nd	nd	nd	nd
1,1,1,2-Tetrachloroethane	0.03	nd	nd	nd	nd	nd	nd	nd
1,1,2,2-Tetrachloroethane	0.02	nd	nd	nd	nd	nd	nd	nd
Carbon tetrachloride	0.03	nd	nd	nd	nd	nd	nd	nd
Naphthalene and 2-Methyl napthalene[1]	N/A	nd	nd	nd	nd	nd	nd	nd
Naphthalene	0.02	nd	nd	nd	nd	nd	nd	nd
2-Methyl naphthalene	0.02	nd	nd	nd	nd	nd	nd	nd

Table 2. Mass of volatile and semivolatile organic compounds detected in passive soil-gas samplers deployed and recovered in the soil of the former hospital landfill, Fort Gordon, Georgia, July 26–30, 2010.—Continued

[Unrounded data provided by W.L. Gore & Associates, Inc.; MDL, method detection level; μg, micrograms; N/A, not applicable; nd, not detected; bdl, below detection level; E, the reported value for a combined mass should be considered estimated if the mass of any of the individual compounds were reported as bdl; a value of 0.00 (reporting format of W.L. Gore & Associates, Inc.) is reported for a combined mass if the individual compounds included in the combined mass were not detected above method detection levels and at least one of the individual compounds was reported as bdl; samplers 637772, 637773, and 637774 are trip blanks]

Organic compound	MDL (μg)	Sampler 637717	Sampler 637718	Sampler 637719	Sampler 637720	Sampler 637721	Sampler 637722	Sampler 637723
Total petroleum hydrocarbons (TPH)	0.02	11.25	1.19	0.51	21.10	18.30	3.02	5.09
BTEX (gasoline)[1]	N/A	nd	nd	nd	nd	nd	nd	nd
Benzene	0.02	nd	nd	nd	nd	nd	nd	nd
Toluene	0.02	nd	nd	nd	nd	nd	nd	nd
Ethylbenzene	0.02	nd	nd	nd	nd	nd	nd	nd
meta-, *para-*, Xylene	0.03	nd	nd	nd	nd	nd	nd	nd
*ortho-*Xylene	0.02	nd	nd	nd	nd	nd	nd	nd
C_{11}, C_{13}, and C_{15} (diesel)[1]	N/A	nd	nd	nd	nd	10.25	E1.99	1.03
Undecane	0.04	nd	nd	nd	nd	10.04	1.92	0.98
Tridecane	0.02	nd	nd	nd	nd	0.13	bdl	0.05
Pentadecane	0.02	nd	nd	nd	nd	0.08	0.07	nd
Octane	0.02	nd	nd	nd	nd	nd	nd	nd
Methyl *tert-*butyl ether	0.03	nd	nd	nd	nd	nd	nd	nd
Trimethylbenzene[1]	N/A	nd	nd	nd	nd	nd	nd	nd
1,2,4-Trimethylbenzene	0.02	nd	nd	nd	nd	nd	nd	nd
1,3,5-Trimethylbenzene	0.03	nd	nd	nd	nd	nd	nd	nd
1,2-Dichlorobenzene	0.02	nd	nd	nd	nd	nd	nd	nd
1,3-Dichlorobenzene	0.02	nd	nd	nd	nd	nd	nd	nd
1,4-Dichlorobenzene	0.02	nd	nd	nd	nd	nd	nd	nd
Chlorobenzene	0.02	nd	nd	nd	nd	nd	nd	nd
Chloroform	0.02	nd	nd	nd	nd	nd	nd	nd
cis- and *trans-*1,2-Dichloroethene[1]	N/A	0.00	nd	nd	nd	nd	nd	nd
*trans-*1,2-Dichloroethene	0.04	nd	nd	nd	nd	nd	nd	nd
*cis-*1,2-Dichloroethene	0.03	bdl	nd	nd	nd	nd	nd	nd
Trichloroethene	0.02	nd	nd	nd	nd	nd	nd	nd
Tetrachloroethene	0.02	0.03	nd	nd	nd	nd	nd	nd
1,1-Dichloroethane	0.02	nd	nd	nd	nd	nd	nd	nd
1,2-Dichloroethane	0.02	nd	nd	nd	nd	nd	nd	nd
1,1,1-Trichloroethane	0.03	nd	nd	nd	nd	nd	nd	nd
1,1,2-Trichloroethane	0.02	nd	nd	nd	nd	nd	nd	nd
1,1,1,2-Tetrachloroethane	0.03	nd	nd	nd	nd	nd	nd	nd
1,1,2,2-Tetrachloroethane	0.02	nd	nd	nd	nd	nd	nd	nd
Carbon tetrachloride	0.03	nd	nd	nd	nd	nd	nd	nd
Naphthalene and 2-Methyl napthalene[1]	N/A	nd	nd	nd	nd	nd	nd	nd
Naphthalene	0.02	nd	nd	nd	nd	nd	nd	nd
2-Methyl naphthalene	0.02	nd	nd	nd	nd	nd	nd	nd

Table 2   21

Table 2.   Mass of volatile and semivolatile organic compounds detected in passive soil-gas samplers deployed and recovered in the soil of the former hospital landfill, Fort Gordon, Georgia, July 26–30, 2010.—Continued

[Unrounded data provided by W.L. Gore & Associates, Inc.; MDL, method detection level; µg, micrograms; N/A, not applicable; nd, not detected; bdl, below detection level; E, the reported value for a combined mass should be considered estimated if the mass of any of the individual compounds were reported as bdl; a value of 0.00 (reporting format of W.L. Gore & Associates, Inc.) is reported for a combined mass if the individual compounds included in the combined mass were not detected above method detection levels and at least one of the individual compounds was reported as bdl; samplers 637772, 637773, and 637774 are trip blanks]

Organic compound	MDL (µg)	Sampler 637724	Sampler 637725	Sampler 637726	Sampler 637727	Sampler 637728	Sampler 637729	Sampler 637730
Total petroleum hydrocarbons (TPH)	0.02	1.18	11.88	0.12	0.77	0.37	0.19	1.56
BTEX (gasoline)[1]	N/A	nd	0.10	0.03	nd	nd	nd	nd
Benzene	0.02	nd	0.10	0.03	nd	nd	nd	nd
Toluene	0.02	nd	nd	nd	nd	nd	nd	nd
Ethylbenzene	0.02	nd	nd	nd	nd	nd	nd	nd
meta-, *para*-, Xylene	0.03	nd	nd	nd	nd	nd	nd	nd
ortho-Xylene	0.02	nd	nd	nd	nd	nd	nd	nd
C_{11}, C_{13}, and C_{15} (diesel)[1]	N/A	nd	nd	nd	0.00	nd	nd	0.10
Undecane	0.04	nd	nd	nd	bdl	nd	nd	0.10
Tridecane	0.02	nd	nd	nd	nd	nd	nd	nd
Pentadecane	0.02	nd	nd	nd	nd	nd	nd	nd
Octane	0.02	nd	nd	nd	nd	nd	nd	nd
Methyl *tert*-butyl ether	0.03	nd	nd	nd	nd	nd	nd	nd
Trimethylbenzene[1]	N/A	nd	nd	nd	nd	nd	nd	nd
1,2,4-Trimethylbenzene	0.02	nd	nd	nd	nd	nd	nd	nd
1,3,5-Trimethylbenzene	0.03	nd	nd	nd	nd	nd	nd	nd
1,2-Dichlorobenzene	0.02	nd	nd	nd	nd	nd	nd	nd
1,3-Dichlorobenzene	0.02	nd	nd	nd	nd	nd	nd	nd
1,4-Dichlorobenzene	0.02	nd	nd	nd	nd	bdl	nd	nd
Chlorobenzene	0.02	nd	nd	nd	nd	nd	nd	nd
Chloroform	0.02	nd	nd	nd	nd	nd	nd	nd
cis- and *trans*-1,2-Dichloroethene[1]	N/A	nd	nd	nd	nd	nd	nd	nd
trans-1,2-Dichloroethene	0.04	nd	nd	nd	nd	nd	nd	nd
cis-1,2-Dichloroethene	0.03	nd	nd	nd	nd	nd	nd	nd
Trichloroethene	0.02	nd	nd	nd	nd	nd	nd	nd
Tetrachloroethene	0.02	nd	nd	nd	nd	nd	nd	nd
1,1-Dichloroethane	0.02	nd	nd	nd	nd	nd	nd	nd
1,2-Dichloroethane	0.02	nd	nd	nd	nd	nd	nd	nd
1,1,1-Trichloroethane	0.03	nd	nd	nd	nd	nd	nd	nd
1,1,2-Trichloroethane	0.02	nd	nd	nd	nd	nd	nd	nd
1,1,1,2-Tetrachloroethane	0.03	nd	nd	nd	nd	nd	nd	nd
1,1,2,2-Tetrachloroethane	0.02	nd	nd	nd	nd	nd	nd	nd
Carbon tetrachloride	0.03	nd	nd	nd	nd	nd	nd	nd
Naphthalene and 2-Methyl napthalene[1]	N/A	nd	nd	nd	nd	nd	nd	nd
Naphthalene	0.02	nd	nd	nd	nd	nd	nd	nd
2-Methyl naphthalene	0.02	nd	nd	nd	nd	nd	nd	nd

Table 2.   Mass of volatile and semivolatile organic compounds detected in passive soil-gas samplers deployed and recovered in the soil of the former hospital landfill, Fort Gordon, Georgia, July 26–30, 2010.—Continued

[Unrounded data provided by W.L. Gore & Associates, Inc.; MDL, method detection level; μg, micrograms; N/A, not applicable; nd, not detected; bdl, below detection level; E, the reported value for a combined mass should be considered estimated if the mass of any of the individual compounds were reported as bdl; a value of 0.00 (reporting format of W.L. Gore & Associates, Inc.) is reported for a combined mass if the individual compounds included in the combined mass were not detected above method detection levels and at least one of the individual compounds was reported as bdl; samplers 637772, 637773, and 637774 are trip blanks]

Organic compound	MDL (μg)	Sampler 637731	Sampler 637732	Sampler 637733	Sampler 637734	Sampler 637735	Sampler 637736	Sampler 637737
Total petroleum hydrocarbons (TPH)	0.02	12.00	0.39	1.57	0.30	0.93	0.67	1.08
BTEX (gasoline)[1]	N/A	nd	nd	nd	nd	nd	nd	nd
Benzene	0.02	nd	nd	nd	nd	nd	nd	nd
Toluene	0.02	nd	nd	nd	nd	nd	nd	nd
Ethylbenzene	0.02	nd	nd	nd	nd	nd	nd	nd
meta-, *para*-, Xylene	0.03	nd	nd	nd	nd	nd	nd	nd
ortho-Xylene	0.02	nd	nd	nd	nd	nd	nd	nd
C_{11}, C_{13}, and C_{15} (diesel)[1]	N/A	nd	nd	nd	nd	nd	nd	nd
Undecane	0.04	nd	nd	nd	nd	nd	nd	nd
Tridecane	0.02	nd	nd	nd	nd	nd	nd	nd
Pentadecane	0.02	nd	nd	nd	nd	nd	nd	nd
Octane	0.02	nd	nd	nd	nd	nd	nd	nd
Methyl *tert*-butyl ether	0.03	nd	nd	nd	nd	nd	nd	nd
Trimethylbenzene[1]	N/A	nd	nd	nd	nd	nd	nd	nd
1,2,4-Trimethylbenzene	0.02	nd	nd	nd	nd	nd	nd	nd
1,3,5-Trimethylbenzene	0.03	nd	nd	nd	nd	nd	nd	nd
1,2-Dichlorobenzene	0.02	nd	nd	nd	nd	nd	nd	nd
1,3-Dichlorobenzene	0.02	nd	nd	nd	nd	nd	nd	nd
1,4-Dichlorobenzene	0.02	nd	nd	nd	nd	nd	nd	nd
Chlorobenzene	0.02	nd	nd	nd	nd	nd	nd	nd
Chloroform	0.02	nd	nd	nd	nd	nd	nd	nd
cis- and *trans*-1,2-Dichloroethene[1]	N/A	nd	nd	nd	nd	nd	nd	nd
trans-1,2-Dichloroethene	0.04	nd	nd	nd	nd	nd	nd	nd
cis-1,2-Dichloroethene	0.03	nd	nd	nd	nd	nd	nd	nd
Trichloroethene	0.02	nd	nd	nd	nd	nd	nd	nd
Tetrachloroethene	0.02	nd	nd	nd	nd	nd	nd	nd
1,1-Dichloroethane	0.02	nd	nd	nd	nd	nd	nd	nd
1,2-Dichloroethane	0.02	nd	nd	nd	nd	nd	nd	nd
1,1,1-Trichloroethane	0.03	nd	nd	nd	nd	nd	nd	nd
1,1,2-Trichloroethane	0.02	nd	nd	nd	nd	nd	nd	nd
1,1,1,2-Tetrachloroethane	0.03	nd	nd	nd	nd	nd	nd	nd
1,1,2,2-Tetrachloroethane	0.02	nd	nd	nd	nd	nd	nd	nd
Carbon tetrachloride	0.03	nd	nd	nd	nd	nd	nd	nd
Naphthalene and 2-Methyl napthalene[1]	N/A	nd	nd	nd	nd	nd	nd	nd
Naphthalene	0.02	nd	nd	nd	nd	nd	nd	nd
2-Methyl naphthalene	0.02	nd	nd	nd	nd	nd	nd	nd

Table 2   23

Table 2. Mass of volatile and semivolatile organic compounds detected in passive soil-gas samplers deployed and recovered in the soil of the former hospital landfill, Fort Gordon, Georgia, July 26–30, 2010.—Continued

[Unrounded data provided by W L. Gore & Associates, Inc.; MDL, method detection level; µg, micrograms; N/A, not applicable; nd, not detected; bdl, below detection level; E, the reported value for a combined mass should be considered estimated if the mass of any of the individual compounds were reported as bdl; a value of 0.00 (reporting format of W.L. Gore & Associates, Inc.) is reported for a combined mass if the individual compounds included in the combined mass were not detected above method detection levels and at least one of the individual compounds was reported as bdl; samplers 637772, 637773, and 637774 are trip blanks]

Organic compound	MDL (µg)	Sampler 637738	Sampler 637739	Sampler 637740	Sampler 637741	Sampler 637742	Sampler 637743	Sampler 637744
Total petroleum hydrocarbons (TPH)	0.02	1.23	0.23	1.77	0.29	1.25	1.05	0.56
BTEX (gasoline)[1]	N/A	nd	nd	nd	nd	nd	nd	0.06
Benzene	0.02	nd	nd	nd	nd	nd	nd	0.06
Toluene	0.02	nd	nd	nd	nd	nd	nd	nd
Ethylbenzene	0.02	nd	nd	nd	nd	nd	nd	nd
meta-, *para-*, Xylene	0.03	nd	nd	nd	nd	nd	nd	nd
*ortho-*Xylene	0.02	nd	nd	nd	nd	nd	nd	nd
C_{11}, C_{13}, and C_{15} (diesel)[1]	N/A	nd	nd	nd	nd	nd	nd	nd
Undecane	0.04	nd	nd	nd	nd	nd	nd	nd
Tridecane	0.02	nd	nd	nd	nd	nd	nd	nd
Pentadecane	0.02	nd	nd	nd	nd	nd	nd	nd
Octane	0.02	nd	nd	nd	nd	nd	nd	nd
Methyl *tert*-butyl ether	0.03	nd	nd	nd	nd	nd	nd	nd
Trimethylbenzene[1]	N/A	nd	nd	nd	nd	nd	nd	nd
1,2,4-Trimethylbenzene	0.02	nd	nd	nd	nd	nd	nd	nd
1,3,5-Trimethylbenzene	0.03	nd	nd	nd	nd	nd	nd	nd
1,2-Dichlorobenzene	0.02	nd	nd	nd	nd	nd	nd	nd
1,3-Dichlorobenzene	0.02	nd	nd	nd	nd	nd	nd	nd
1,4-Dichlorobenzene	0.02	nd	nd	nd	nd	nd	nd	nd
Chlorobenzene	0.02	nd	nd	nd	nd	nd	nd	nd
Chloroform	0.02	nd	nd	nd	nd	nd	nd	nd
cis- and *trans-*1,2-Dichloroethene[1]	N/A	nd	nd	nd	nd	nd	nd	nd
*trans-*1,2-Dichloroethene	0.04	nd	nd	nd	nd	nd	nd	nd
*cis-*1,2-Dichloroethene	0.03	nd	nd	nd	nd	nd	nd	nd
Trichloroethene	0.02	nd	nd	nd	nd	nd	nd	nd
Tetrachloroethene	0.02	nd	nd	nd	nd	nd	nd	nd
1,1-Dichloroethane	0.02	nd	nd	nd	nd	nd	nd	nd
1,2-Dichloroethane	0.02	nd	nd	nd	nd	nd	nd	nd
1,1,1-Trichloroethane	0.03	nd	nd	nd	nd	nd	nd	nd
1,1,2-Trichloroethane	0.02	nd	nd	nd	nd	nd	nd	nd
1,1,1,2-Tetrachloroethane	0.03	nd	nd	nd	nd	nd	nd	nd
1,1,2,2-Tetrachloroethane	0.02	nd	nd	nd	nd	nd	nd	nd
Carbon tetrachloride	0.03	nd	nd	nd	nd	nd	nd	nd
Naphthalene and 2-Methyl napthalene[1]	N/A	nd	nd	nd	nd	nd	nd	nd
Naphthalene	0.02	nd	nd	nd	nd	nd	nd	nd
2-Methyl naphthalene	0.02	nd	nd	nd	nd	nd	nd	nd

Table 2. Mass of volatile and semivolatile organic compounds detected in passive soil-gas samplers deployed and recovered in the soil of the former hospital landfill, Fort Gordon, Georgia, July 26–30, 2010.—Continued

[Unrounded data provided by W.L. Gore & Associates, Inc.; MDL, method detection level; μg, micrograms; N/A, not applicable; nd, not detected; bdl, below detection level; E, the reported value for a combined mass should be considered estimated if the mass of any of the individual compounds were reported as bdl; a value of 0.00 (reporting format of W.L. Gore & Associates, Inc.) is reported for a combined mass if the individual compounds included in the combined mass were not detected above method detection levels and at least one of the individual compounds was reported as bdl; samplers 637772, 637773, and 637774 are trip blanks]

Organic compound	MDL (μg)	Sampler 637745	Sampler 637746	Sampler 637747	Sampler 637748	Sampler 637749	Sampler 637750	Sampler 637751
Total petroleum hydrocarbons (TPH)	0.02	27.94	0.13	1.40	0.97	0.57	0.08	0.36
BTEX (gasoline)[1]	N/A	0.14	nd	nd	nd	nd	nd	nd
Benzene	0.02	nd	nd	nd	nd	nd	nd	nd
Toluene	0.02	0.14	nd	nd	nd	nd	nd	nd
Ethylbenzene	0.02	nd	nd	nd	nd	nd	nd	nd
meta-, *para-*, Xylene	0.03	nd	nd	nd	nd	nd	nd	nd
ortho-Xylene	0.02	nd	nd	nd	nd	nd	nd	nd
C_{11}, C_{13}, and C_{15} (diesel)[1]	N/A	nd	nd	0.00	nd	0.00	nd	nd
Undecane	0.04	nd	nd	bdl	nd	bdl	nd	nd
Tridecane	0.02	nd	nd	nd	nd	nd	nd	nd
Pentadecane	0.02	nd	nd	nd	nd	nd	nd	nd
Octane	0.02	nd	nd	nd	nd	nd	nd	nd
Methyl *tert*-butyl ether	0.03	nd	nd	nd	nd	nd	nd	nd
Trimethylbenzene[1]	N/A	nd	nd	nd	nd	nd	nd	nd
1,2,4-Trimethylbenzene	0.02	nd	nd	nd	nd	nd	nd	nd
1,3,5-Trimethylbenzene	0.03	nd	nd	nd	nd	nd	nd	nd
1,2-Dichlorobenzene	0.02	nd	nd	nd	nd	nd	nd	nd
1,3-Dichlorobenzene	0.02	nd	nd	nd	nd	nd	nd	nd
1,4-Dichlorobenzene	0.02	nd	nd	nd	nd	nd	nd	nd
Chlorobenzene	0.02	nd	nd	nd	nd	nd	nd	nd
Chloroform	0.02	nd	nd	nd	nd	nd	nd	nd
cis- and *trans*-1,2-Dichloroethene[1]	N/A	nd	nd	nd	nd	nd	nd	nd
trans-1,2-Dichloroethene	0.04	nd	nd	nd	nd	nd	nd	nd
cis-1,2-Dichloroethene	0.03	nd	nd	nd	nd	nd	nd	nd
Trichloroethene	0.02	nd	nd	nd	nd	nd	nd	nd
Tetrachloroethene	0.02	nd	nd	nd	nd	nd	0.06	nd
1,1-Dichloroethane	0.02	nd	nd	nd	nd	nd	nd	nd
1,2-Dichloroethane	0.02	nd	nd	nd	nd	nd	nd	nd
1,1,1-Trichloroethane	0.03	nd	nd	nd	nd	nd	nd	nd
1,1,2-Trichloroethane	0.02	nd	nd	nd	nd	nd	nd	nd
1,1,1,2-Tetrachloroethane	0.03	nd	nd	nd	nd	nd	nd	nd
1,1,2,2-Tetrachloroethane	0.02	nd	nd	nd	nd	nd	nd	nd
Carbon tetrachloride	0.03	nd	nd	nd	nd	nd	nd	nd
Naphthalene and 2-Methyl napthalene[1]	N/A	nd	nd	nd	nd	nd	nd	nd
Naphthalene	0.02	nd	nd	nd	nd	nd	nd	nd
2-Methyl naphthalene	0.02	nd	nd	nd	nd	nd	nd	nd

Table 2   25

Table 2.   Mass of volatile and semivolatile organic compounds detected in passive soil-gas samplers deployed and recovered in the soil of the former hospital landfill, Fort Gordon, Georgia, July 26–30, 2010.—Continued

[Unrounded data provided by W.L. Gore & Associates, Inc.; MDL, method detection level; μg, micrograms; N/A, not applicable; nd, not detected; bdl, below detection level; E, the reported value for a combined mass should be considered estimated if the mass of any of the individual compounds were reported as bdl; a value of 0.00 (reporting format of W.L. Gore & Associates, Inc.) is reported for a combined mass if the individual compounds included in the combined mass were not detected above method detection levels and at least one of the individual compounds was reported as bdl; samplers 637772, 637773, and 637774 are trip blanks]

Organic compound	MDL (μg)	Sampler 637752	Sampler 637753	Sampler 637754	Sampler 637755	Sampler 637756	Sampler 637757
Total petroleum hydrocarbons (TPH)	0.02	0.10	14.44	0.24	4.05	0.92	2.23
BTEX (gasoline)[1]	N/A	nd	nd	nd	nd	nd	nd
Benzene	0.02	nd	nd	nd	nd	nd	nd
Toluene	0.02	nd	nd	nd	nd	nd	nd
Ethylbenzene	0.02	nd	nd	nd	nd	nd	nd
meta-, para-, Xylene	0.03	nd	nd	nd	nd	nd	nd
ortho-Xylene	0.02	nd	nd	nd	nd	nd	nd
C_{11}, C_{13}, and C_{15} (diesel)[1]	N/A	nd	0.55	nd	0.20	0.20	0.12
Undecane	0.04	nd	0.50	nd	0.20	0.20	0.12
Tridecane	0.02	nd	0.05	nd	nd	nd	nd
Pentadecane	0.02	nd	nd	nd	nd	nd	nd
Octane	0.02	nd	nd	nd	nd	nd	nd
Methyl tert-butyl ether	0.03	nd	nd	nd	nd	nd	nd
Trimethylbenzene[1]	N/A	nd	nd	nd	nd	nd	nd
1,2,4-Trimethylbenzene	0.02	nd	nd	nd	nd	nd	nd
1,3,5-Trimethylbenzene	0.03	nd	nd	nd	nd	nd	nd
1,2-Dichlorobenzene	0.02	nd	nd	nd	nd	nd	nd
1,3-Dichlorobenzene	0.02	nd	nd	nd	nd	nd	nd
1,4-Dichlorobenzene	0.02	nd	nd	nd	nd	nd	nd
Chlorobenzene	0.02	nd	nd	nd	nd	nd	nd
Chloroform	0.02	nd	nd	nd	nd	nd	nd
cis- and trans-1,2-Dichloroethene[1]	N/A	nd	nd	nd	nd	nd	nd
trans-1,2-Dichloroethene	0.04	nd	nd	nd	nd	nd	nd
cis-1,2-Dichloroethene	0.03	nd	nd	nd	nd	nd	nd
Trichloroethene	0.02	nd	nd	nd	nd	nd	nd
Tetrachloroethene	0.02	nd	nd	nd	nd	nd	0.21
1,1-Dichloroethane	0.02	nd	nd	nd	nd	nd	nd
1,2-Dichloroethane	0.02	nd	nd	nd	nd	nd	nd
1,1,1-Trichloroethane	0.03	nd	nd	nd	nd	nd	nd
1,1,2-Trichloroethane	0.02	nd	nd	nd	nd	nd	nd
1,1,1,2-Tetrachloroethane	0.03	nd	nd	nd	nd	nd	nd
1,1,2,2-Tetrachloroethane	0.02	nd	nd	nd	nd	nd	nd
Carbon tetrachloride	0.03	nd	nd	nd	nd	nd	nd
Naphthalene and 2-Methyl napthalene[1]	N/A	nd	nd	nd	nd	nd	nd
Naphthalene	0.02	nd	nd	nd	nd	nd	nd
2-Methyl naphthalene	0.02	nd	nd	nd	nd	nd	nd

Table 2.   Mass of volatile and semivolatile organic compounds detected in passive soil-gas samplers deployed and recovered in the soil of the former hospital landfill, Fort Gordon, Georgia, July 26–30, 2010.—Continued

[Unrounded data provided by W.L. Gore & Associates, Inc.; MDL, method detection level; μg, micrograms; N/A, not applicable; nd, not detected; bdl, below detection level; E, the reported value for a combined mass should be considered estimated if the mass of any of the individual compounds were reported as bdl; a value of 0.00 (reporting format of W.L. Gore & Associates, Inc.) is reported for a combined mass if the individual compounds included in the combined mass were not detected above method detection levels and at least one of the individual compounds was reported as bdl; samplers 637772, 637773, and 637774 are trip blanks]

Organic compound	MDL (μg)	Sampler 637758	Sampler 637759	Sampler 637760	Sampler 637761
Total petroleum hydrocarbons (TPH)	0.02	0.26	1.96	31.72	0.90
BTEX (gasoline)[1]	N/A	nd	nd	nd	nd
Benzene	0.02	nd	nd	nd	nd
Toluene	0.02	nd	nd	nd	nd
Ethylbenzene	0.02	nd	nd	nd	nd
meta-, *para*-, Xylene	0.03	nd	nd	nd	nd
ortho-Xylene	0.02	nd	nd	nd	nd
C_{11}, C_{13}, and C_{15} (diesel)[1]	N/A	nd	nd	24.41	nd
Undecane	0.04	nd	nd	22.84	nd
Tridecane	0.02	nd	nd	0.60	nd
Pentadecane	0.02	nd	nd	0.97	nd
Octane	0.02	nd	nd	nd	nd
Methyl *tert*-butyl ether	0.03	nd	nd	nd	nd
Trimethylbenzene[1]	N/A	nd	nd	nd	nd
1,2,4-Trimethylbenzene	0.02	nd	nd	nd	nd
1,3,5-Trimethylbenzene	0.03	nd	nd	nd	nd
1,2-Dichlorobenzene	0.02	nd	nd	nd	nd
1,3-Dichlorobenzene	0.02	nd	nd	nd	nd
1,4-Dichlorobenzene	0.02	nd	nd	nd	nd
Chlorobenzene	0.02	nd	nd	nd	nd
Chloroform	0.02	nd	nd	nd	nd
cis- and *trans*-1,2-Dichloroethene[1]	N/A	nd	nd	nd	nd
trans-1,2-Dichloroethene	0.04	nd	nd	nd	nd
cis-1,2-Dichloroethene	0.03	nd	nd	nd	nd
Trichloroethene	0.02	nd	nd	nd	nd
Tetrachloroethene	0.02	nd	nd	nd	nd
1,1-Dichloroethane	0.02	nd	nd	nd	nd
1,2-Dichloroethane	0.02	nd	nd	nd	nd
1,1,1-Trichloroethane	0.03	nd	nd	nd	nd
1,1,2-Trichloroethane	0.02	nd	nd	nd	nd
1,1,1,2-Tetrachloroethane	0.03	nd	nd	nd	nd
1,1,2,2-Tetrachloroethane	0.02	nd	nd	nd	nd
Carbon tetrachloride	0.03	nd	nd	nd	nd
Naphthalene and 2-Methyl napthalene[1]	N/A	nd	nd	nd	nd
Naphthalene	0.02	nd	nd	nd	nd
2-Methyl naphthalene	0.02	nd	nd	nd	nd

Table 2   27

Table 2. Mass of volatile and semivolatile organic compounds detected in passive soil-gas samplers deployed and recovered in the soil of the former hospital landfill, Fort Gordon, Georgia, July 26–30, 2010.—Continued

[Unrounded data provided by W.L. Gore & Associates, Inc.; MDL, method detection level; µg, micrograms; N/A, not applicable; nd, not detected; bdl, below detection level; E, the reported value for a combined mass should be considered estimated if the mass of any of the individual compounds were reported as bdl; a value of 0.00 (reporting format of W.L. Gore & Associates, Inc.) is reported for a combined mass if the individual compounds included in the combined mass were not detected above method detection levels and at least one of the individual compounds was reported as bdl; samplers 637772, 637773, and 637774 are trip blanks]

Organic compound	MDL (µg)	Sampler 637772	Sampler 637773	Sampler 637774	Method blank	Method blank
Total petroleum hydrocarbons (TPH)	0.02	bdl	nd	bdl	bdl	nd
BTEX (gasoline)[1]	N/A	nd	nd	nd	nd	nd
Benzene	0.02	nd	nd	nd	nd	nd
Toluene	0.02	nd	nd	nd	nd	nd
Ethylbenzene	0.02	nd	nd	nd	nd	nd
meta-, *para*-, Xylene	0.03	nd	nd	nd	nd	nd
ortho-Xylene	0.02	nd	nd	nd	nd	nd
C_{11}, C_{13}, and C_{15} (diesel)[1]	N/A	nd	nd	nd	nd	nd
Undecane	0.04	nd	nd	nd	nd	nd
Tridecane	0.02	nd	nd	nd	nd	nd
Pentadecane	0.02	nd	nd	nd	nd	nd
Octane	0.02	nd	nd	nd	nd	nd
Methyl *tert*-butyl ether	0.03	nd	nd	nd	nd	nd
Trimethylbenzene[1]	N/A	nd	nd	nd	nd	nd
1,2,4-Trimethylbenzene	0.02	nd	nd	nd	nd	nd
1,3,5-Trimethylbenzene	0.03	nd	nd	nd	nd	nd
1,2-Dichlorobenzene	0.02	nd	nd	nd	nd	nd
1,3-Dichlorobenzene	0.02	nd	nd	nd	nd	nd
1,4-Dichlorobenzene	0.02	nd	nd	nd	nd	nd
Chlorobenzene	0.02	nd	nd	nd	nd	nd
Chloroform	0.02	nd	nd	nd	nd	nd
cis- and *trans*-1,2-Dichloroethene[1]	N/A	nd	nd	nd	nd	nd
trans-1,2-Dichloroethene	0.04	nd	nd	nd	nd	nd
cis-1,2-Dichloroethene	0.03	nd	nd	nd	nd	nd
Trichloroethene	0.02	0.03	nd	nd	nd	nd
Tetrachloroethene	0.02	0.08	nd	nd	nd	nd
1,1-Dichloroethane	0.02	nd	nd	nd	nd	nd
1,2-Dichloroethane	0.02	nd	nd	nd	nd	nd
1,1,1-Trichloroethane	0.03	nd	nd	nd	nd	nd
1,1,2-Trichloroethane	0.02	nd	nd	nd	nd	nd
1,1,1,2-Tetrachloroethane	0.03	nd	nd	nd	nd	nd
1,1,2,2-Tetrachloroethane	0.02	nd	nd	nd	nd	nd
Carbon tetrachloride	0.03	nd	nd	nd	nd	nd
Naphthalene and 2-Methyl napthalene[1]	N/A	nd	nd	nd	nd	nd
Naphthalene	0.02	nd	nd	nd	nd	nd
2-Methyl naphthalene	0.02	nd	nd	nd	nd	nd

[1] Combined mass for two or more compounds with no method detection level provided by laboratory.

Table 3.   Mass of chemical agents and explosives classified as volatile and semivolatile organic compounds detected in passive soil-gas samples deployed and collected in the soil of the former hospital landfill, Fort Gordon, Georgia, September 16–22, 2010.

[Unrounded data provided by W.L. Gore & Associates, Inc.; MDL, method detection level; μg, micrograms; nd, not detected; bdl, below detection level; closest July sampler number in brackets (fig. 12); samplers 644252 through 644256 are trip blanks]

	MDL (μg)	Sampler 644230 [637736]	Sampler 644231 [637716]	Sampler 644232 [637718]	Sampler 644233 [637721]	Sampler 644234 [637760]	Method blank
Chemical agents							
Dimethyl disulfide	0.10	nd	nd	nd	nd	nd	nd
Dimethyl methylphosphonate	0.10	nd	nd	nd	nd	nd	nd
1,4-Thioxane	0.10	nd	nd	nd	nd	nd	nd
Diisopropyl methylphosphonate	0.10	nd	nd	nd	nd	nd	nd
1,4-Dithiane	0.10	nd	nd	nd	nd	nd	nd
Thiodiglycol	0.20	nd	nd	nd	nd	nd	nd
Benzothiazole	0.10	nd	bdl	bdl	nd	bdl	nd
Chloroacetophenones	0.10	nd	nd	nd	nd	0.13	nd
para-Chlorophenyl methyl sulfide	0.10	nd	nd	bdl	nd	nd	bdl
para-Chlorophenyl methyl sulfoxide	0.10	nd	nd	nd	nd	nd	bdl
para-Chlorophenyl methyl sulfone	0.10	bdl	bdl	bdl	bdl	bdl	bdl
Explosives							
Nitrobenzene	0.10	nd	nd	nd	nd	nd	nd
1,3-Dinitrobenzene	0.10	nd	nd	nd	nd	nd	bdl
1,3,5-Trinitrobenzene	0.10	nd	nd	nd	nd	nd	nd
2-Nitrotoluene	0.10	nd	nd	nd	nd	nd	nd
3-Nitrotoluene	0.10	nd	nd	nd	nd	nd	nd
4-Nitrotoluene	0.10	nd	nd	nd	nd	nd	nd
2,4-Dinitrotoluene	0.10	nd	nd	nd	nd	nd	bdl
2,6-Dinitrotoluene	0.10	nd	nd	nd	nd	nd	bdl
2,4,6-Trinitrotoluene	0.10	nd	nd	nd	nd	nd	nd

Table 3   29

Table 3. Mass of chemical agents and explosives classified as volatile and semivolatile organic compounds detected in passive soil-gas samples deployed and collected in the soil of the former hospital landfill, Fort Gordon, Georgia, September 16–22, 2010.—Continued

[Unrounded data provided by W L. Gore & Associates, Inc.; MDL, method detection level; μg, micrograms; nd, not detected; bdl, below detection level; closest July sampler number in brackets (fig. 12); samplers 644252 through 644256 are trip blanks]

	MDL (μg)	Method blank	Method blank	Sampler 644252	Sampler 644253	Sampler 644254	Sampler 644255	Sampler 644256
Chemical agents								
Dimethyl disulfide	0.10	nd	nd	nd	nd	nd	nd	nd
Dimethyl methylphosphonate	0.10	nd	nd	nd	nd	nd	nd	nd
1,4-Thioxane	0.10	nd	nd	nd	nd	nd	nd	nd
Diisopropyl methylphosphonate	0.10	nd	nd	nd	nd	nd	nd	nd
1,4-Dithiane	0.10	nd	nd	nd	nd	nd	nd	nd
Thiodiglycol	0.20	nd	nd	nd	nd	nd	nd	nd
Benzothiazole	0.10	nd	nd	nd	nd	nd	nd	nd
Chloroacetophenones	0.10	nd	nd	nd	nd	nd	nd	nd
para-Chlorophenyl methyl sulfide	0.10	nd	nd	nd	nd	nd	nd	nd
para-Chlorophenyl methyl sulfoxide	0.10	nd	nd	nd	nd	nd	nd	nd
para-Chlorophenyl methyl sulfone	0.10	bdl	bdl	bdl	bdl	bdl	bdl	bdl
Explosives								
Nitrobenzene	0.10	nd	nd	nd	nd	nd	nd	nd
1,3-Dinitrobenzene	0.10	nd	nd	nd	nd	nd	nd	nd
1,3,5-Trinitrobenzene	0.10	nd	nd	nd	nd	nd	nd	nd
2-Nitrotoluene	0.10	nd	nd	nd	nd	nd	nd	nd
3-Nitrotoluene	0.10	nd	bdl	nd	nd	nd	nd	nd
4-Nitrotoluene	0.10	nd	nd	nd	nd	nd	nd	nd
2,4-Dinitrotoluene	0.10	nd	nd	nd	nd	nd	nd	bdl
2,6-Dinitrotoluene	0.10	bdl	nd	nd	nd	nd	nd	nd
2,4,6-Trinitrotoluene	0.10	nd	nd	nd	nd	nd	nd	nd

Table 4.   Inorganic constituents detected in soil samples 1–5 collected from land surface to a depth of 6 inches at the former hospital landfill, Fort Gordon, Georgia, August 30, 2010.

[USEPA RSL, U.S. Environmental Protection Agency Regional Screening Level, Industrial Soil; mg/kg, milligrams per kilogram; μg/g, micrograms per gram; SCDHEC, South Carolina Department of Health and Environmental Control; <, less than; for soil, 1 μg/g is equivalent to 1 mg/kg, and 1 mg/kg is equivalent to 1 part per million (ppm); N/A, not applicable; yellow highlight, higher than South Carolina background; Note: selenium and mercury were not analyzed; *, Resource Conservation and Recovery Act (RCRA) metal]

[Closest July Soil-Gas Sampler]	Sample 1 (3325520 82081300) (μg/g) [637760]	Sample 2 (3325520 82080900) (μg/g) [637736]	Sample 3 (3325580 82080700) (μg/g) [637716]	Sample 4 (3326010 82080700) (μg/g) [637718]	Sample 5 (3326040 82080700) (μg/g) [637721]	US EPA RSL (mg/kg)	SCDHEC Background (mg/kg)
Inorganic constituents							
Aluminum	15,900	11,900	2,770	19,300	18,500	990,000	13,528
Antimony	0.2	0.58	0.1	0.1	0.09	410	N/A
Arsenic*	1.9	2.7	<1	<1	<1	260	6.1
Barium*	93.9	116	94.4	77.6	75.9	190,000	38
Beryllium	0.34	0.5	0.15	0.31	0.29	2,000	0.6
Cadmium*	<0.007	0.04	<0.007	0.01	0.008	800	1
Calcium	<100	415	<100	162	178	N/A	699
Cerium	25.2	28.8	10.6	37.6	53.8	N/A	N/A
Cesium	0.67	0.67	0.14	0.5	0.44	N/A	N/A
Chromium*	16.8	10.6	3.5	9.3	9.7	1,500,000	16
Cobalt	0.79	1.2	0.15	0.76	0.58	300	4
Copper	5.1	7	<2	3.6	3.9	41,000	9
Gallium	3.7	3.1	0.79	4.5	5	N/A	N/A
Iron	5,150	5,050	2,210	2,400	2,930	720,000	15,608
Lanthanum	12	10.9	3.8	17.2	25.1	N/A	N/A
Lead*	6.29	19.3	2.86	6.45	6.21	800	16
Lithium	5.1	7.1	4.5	6.5	5.5	2,000	N/A
Magnesium	332	419	90.1	279	285	N/A	988
Manganese	39.8	31.6	4.9	78.6	52.7	23,000	120
Molybdenum	0.26	0.39	0.09	0.2	0.2	5,100	N/A
Nickel	3.1	4.3	0.7	3.2	2.4	47,000	6
Niobium	3.2	2.4	0.46	2.9	5.3	N/A	N/A
Phosphorus	152	168	111	96.1	95	N/A	N/A
Potassium	683	745	126	2,010	2,290	N/A	856
Rubidium	6.2	6	1.2	13	13.7	N/A	N/A
Scandium	1.9	1.8	0.6	2.1	2.6	N/A	N/A
Silver*	0.013	0.049	<0.01	<0.01	<0.01	5,100	4
Sodium	65.7	133	26.6	199	231	N/A	194
Strontium	15.2	36.4	14	8	7.2	610,000	N/A
Thallium	<0.08	0.19	<0.08	0.09	<0.08	N/A	4.5
Thorium	4.01	2.5	0.67	5.53	11	N/A	N/A
Uranium	1.33	0.99	0.52	0.92	1.99	N/A	N/A
Vanadium	19.3	17.5	3.9	13.6	15.9	5,200	N/A
Yttrium	2.4	3.8	1.2	3.5	4.2	N/A	N/A
Zinc	10.6	23.4	< 3	7.6	9.7	310,000	23

Table 5   31

Table 5.   Field parameters and analytical results for an unfiltered surface-water sample collected from the unnamed tributary to Butler Creek adjacent to the former hospital landfill, Fort Gordon, Georgia, September 8, 2010.

[id., identification; USEPA NPDWS (*NSDWS*), U.S. Environmental Protection Agency National Primary Drinking Water Standard (*National Secondary Drinking Water Standard*); ---, no trip blank results; µS/cm, microsiemens per centimeters at 25 degrees Celsius; s.u., standard pH units; mg/L, milligrams per liter; °C, degrees Celsius; <, less than; E, estimated; µg/L, micrograms per liter; icp, inductively coupled plasma; cicp, cell inductively coupled plasma; ms, mass spectrometry; lle, liquid-liquid extraction; p&t, purge and trap; gcms, gas chromatography mass spectrometry; N/A, not applicable; pct, percent]

	Downstream site id. 332608082080400	Trip blank id. 332443082064600	Units	Method	USEPA NPDWS (*NSDWS*)
Field parameters					
Specific conductance	32	---	µS/cm	meter	N/A
Specific conductance (lab)	33	---	µS/cm	meter	N/A
pH	6.1	---	s.u.	meter	N/A
Dissolved oxygen	7.6	---	mg/L	meter	N/A
Temperature	23.2	---	°C	meter	N/A
Inorganic constituents					
Aluminum	59	---	µg/L	icp-ms	*50 to 200*
Arsenic	0.3	---	µg/L	cicp-ms	10
Barium	14.6	---	µg/L	icp	2,000
Beryllium	<0.38	---	µg/L	icp	4
Cadmium	E0.03	---	µg/L	icp-ms	5
Calcium	2.45	---	mg/L	icp	N/A
Chromium	E0.38	---	µg/L	cicp-ms	100
Cobalt	0.08	---	µg/L	cicp-ms	N/A
Copper	<4	---	µg/L	icp	*1,000*
Iron	1,340	---	µg/L	icp	*300*
Lead	0.47	---	µg/L	icp-ms	N/A
Lithium	1	---	µg/L	icp	N/A
Magnesium	0.63	---	mg/L	icp	N/A
Manganese	7.5	---	µg/L	icp	*50*
Molybdenum	E0.1	---	µg/L	icp-ms	N/A
Nickel	E0.18	---	µg/L	cicp-ms	N/A
Potassium	0.28	---	mg/L	icp	N/A
Selenium	E0.09	---	µg/L	cicp-ms	50
Silver	<0.02	---	µg/L	icp-ms	*100*
Sodium	2.1	---	mg/L	icp	N/A
Strontium	15.4	---	µg/L	icp	N/A
Zinc	5	---	µg/L	icp	*5,000*

Table 5. Field parameters and analytical results for an unfiltered surface-water sample collected from the unnamed tributary to Butler Creek adjacent to the former hospital landfill, Fort Gordon, Georgia, September 8, 2010.—Continued

[id , identification; USEPA NPDWS (*NSDWS*), United States Environmental Protection Agency National Primary Drinking Water Standard (*National Secondary Drinking Water Standard*); ---, no trip blank results; µS/cm, microsiemens per centimeters at 25 degrees Celsius; s.u., standard pH units; mg/L, milligrams per liter; °C, degrees Celsius; <, less than; E, estimated; µg/L, micrograms per liter; icp, inductively coupled plasma; cicp, cell inductively coupled plasma; ms, mass spectrometry; lle, liquid-liquid extraction; p&t, purge and trap; gcms, gas chromatography mass spectrometry; N/A, not applicable; pct, percent]

	Downstream site id. 332608082080400	Trip blank id. 332443082064600	Units	Method	USEPA NPDWS (*NSDWS*)
Volatile organic compounds					
1,1,1,2-Tetrachloroethane	<0.04	<0.04	µg/L	p&t gcms	N/A
1,1,1-Trichloroethane	<0.03	<0.03	µg/L	p&t gcms	200
1,1,2,2-Tetrachloroethane	<0.14	<0.14	µg/L	p&t gcms	N/A
1,1,2-Trichloroethane	<0.05	<0.05	µg/L	p&t gcms	5
1,1,2-Trichlorotrifluoroethane	<0.03	<0.03	µg/L	p&t gcms	N/A
1,1-Dichloroethane	<0.04	<0.04	µg/L	p&t gcms	N/A
1,1-Dichloroethylene	<0.02	<0.02	µg/L	p&t gcms	7
1,1-Dichloropropene	<0.03	<0.03	µg/L	p&t gcms	N/A
1,2,3,4-Tetramethylbenzene	<0.1	<0.1	µg/L	p&t gcms	N/A
1,2,3,5-Tetramethylbenzene	<0.1	<0.1	µg/L	p&t gcms	N/A
1,2,3-Trichlorobenzene	<0.1	<0.1	µg/L	p&t gcms	N/A
1,2,3-Trichloropropane	<0.12	<0.12	µg/L	p&t gcms	N/A
1,2,3-Trimethylbenzene	<0.1	<0.1	µg/L	p&t gcms	N/A
1,2,4-Trichlorobenzene	<0.1	<0.1	µg/L	p&t gcms	70
1,2,4-Trimethylbenzene	<0.03	<0.03	µg/L	p&t gcms	N/A
1,2-Dibromo-3-chloropropane	<0.3	<0.3	µg/L	p&t gcms	0.2
1,2-Dibromoethane	<0.05	<0.05	µg/L	p&t gcms	N/A
1,2-Dichlorobenzene	<0.03	<0.03	µg/L	p&t gcms	N/A
1,2-Dichloroethane	<0.1	<0.1	µg/L	p&t gcms	5
1,2-Dichloropropane	<0.03	<0.03	µg/L	p&t gcms	5
1,3,5-Trimethylbenzene	<0.03	<0.03	µg/L	p&t gcms	N/A
1,3-Dichlorobenzene	<0.02	<0.02	µg/L	p&t gcms	N/A
1,3-Dichloropropane	<0.1	<0.1	µg/L	p&t gcms	N/A
1,4-Dichlorobenzene	<0.03	<0.03	µg/L	p&t gcms	N/A
2,2-Dichloropropane	<0.06	<0.06	µg/L	p&t gcms	N/A
2-Butanone	<1.6	<1.6	µg/L	p&t gcms	N/A
2-Chlorotoluene	<0.03	<0.03	µg/L	p&t gcms	N/A
2-Hexanone	<0.5	<0.5	µg/L	p&t gcms	N/A
3-Chloropropene	<0.08	<0.08	µg/L	p&t gcms	N/A
4-Chlorotoluene	<0.04	<0.04	µg/L	p&t gcms	N/A
4-Isopropyl-1-Methylbenzene	<0.06	<0.06	µg/L	p&t gcms	N/A
4-Methyl-2-pentanone	<0.3	<0.3	µg/L	p&t gcms	N/A
Acetone	<3	<3	µg/L	p&t gcms	N/A
Acrylonitrile	<0.8	<0.8	µg/L	p&t gcms	N/A
Benzene	<0.03	<0.03	µg/L	p&t gcms	5
Bromobenzene	<0.02	<0.02	µg/L	p&t gcms	N/A
Bromochloromethane	<0.06	<0.06	µg/L	p&t gcms	N/A
Bromodichloromethane	<0.03	<0.03	µg/L	p&t gcms	N/A
Bromoethene	<0.1	<0.1	µg/L	p&t gcms	N/A

Table 5   33

Table 5. Field parameters and analytical results for an unfiltered surface-water sample collected from the unnamed tributary to Butler Creek adjacent to the former hospital landfill, Fort Gordon, Georgia, September 8, 2010.—Continued

[id., identification; USEPA NPDWS (*NSDWS*), United States Environmental Protection Agency National Primary Drinking Water Standard (*National Secondary Drinking Water Standard*); ---, no trip blank results; μS/cm, microSiemens per centimeters at 25 degrees Celsius; s.u., standard pH units; mg/L, milligrams per liter; °C, degrees Celsius; <, less than; E, estimated; mg/L, micrograms per liter; icp, inductively coupled plasma; cicp, cell inductively coupled plasma; ms, mass spectrometry; lle, liquid-liquid extraction; p&t, purge and trap; gcms, gas chromatography mass spectrometry; N/A, not applicable; pct, percent]

	Downstream site id. 332608082080400	Trip blank id. 332443082064600	Units	Method	USEPA NPDWS (*NSDWS*)
Volatile organic compounds					
Bromoform	<0.1	<0.1	μg/L	p&t gcms	N/A
Bromomethane	<0.2	<0.2	μg/L	p&t gcms	N/A
Butylbenzene	<0.1	<0.1	μg/L	p&t gcms	N/A
Carbon disulfide	<0.04	<0.04	μg/L	p&t gcms	N/A
Chlorobenzene	<0.02	<0.02	μg/L	p&t gcms	100
Chloroethane	<0.1	<0.1	μg/L	p&t gcms	N/A
Chloroform	E0.02	<0.03	μg/L	p&t gcms	N/A
Chloromethane	<0.1	<0.1	μg/L	p&t gcms	N/A
cis-1,2-Dichloroethylene	<0.02	<0.02	μg/L	p&t gcms	70
cis-1,3-Dichloropropene	<0.1	<0.1	μg/L	p&t gcms	N/A
Dibromochloromethane	<0.1	<0.1	μg/L	p&t gcms	N/A
Dibromomethane	<0.05	<0.05	μg/L	p&t gcms	N/A
Dichlorodifluoromethane	<0.1	<0.1	μg/L	p&t gcms	N/A
Dichloromethane	<0.04	<0.04	μg/L	p&t gcms	5
Diethyl ether	<0.1	<0.1	μg/L	p&t gcms	N/A
Diisopropyl ether	<0.1	<0.1	μg/L	p&t gcms	N/A
Ethyl methacrylate	<0.1	<0.1	μg/L	p&t gcms	N/A
Ethyl *tert*-butyl ether	<0.03	<0.03	μg/L	p&t gcms	N/A
Ethylbenzene	<0.04	<0.04	μg/L	p&t gcms	700
Hexachlorobutadiene	<0.1	<0.1	μg/L	p&t gcms	N/A
Hexachloroethane	<0.1	<0.1	μg/L	p&t gcms	N/A
Isopropylbenzene	<0.04	<0.04	μg/L	p&t gcms	N/A
meta- and *para*-xylene	<0.08	<0.08	μg/L	p&t gcms	10,000
Methyl acrylate	<0.6	<0.6	μg/L	p&t gcms	N/A
Methyl acrylonitrile	<0.3	<0.3	μg/L	p&t gcms	N/A
Methyl iodide	<0.3	<0.3	μg/L	p&t gcms	N/A
Methyl methacrylate	<0.22	<0.22	μg/L	p&t gcms	N/A
Naphthalene	<0.2	<0.2	μg/L	p&t gcms	N/A
normal-Propylbenzene	<0.04	<0.04	μg/L	p&t gcms	N/A
ortho-Ethyl toluene	<0.03	<0.03	μg/L	p&t gcms	N/A
ortho-Xylene	<0.03	<0.03	μg/L	p&t gcms	10,000
sec-Butylbenzene	<0.03	<0.03	μg/L	p&t gcms	N/A
Styrene	<0.03	<0.03	μg/L	p&t gcms	100
tert-Butyl methyl ether	<0.1	<0.1	μg/L	p&t gcms	N/A
tert-Butylbenzene	<0.06	<0.06	μg/L	p&t gcms	N/A
tert-Pentyl methyl ether	<0.06	<0.06	μg/L	p&t gcms	N/A
Tetrachloroethylene	<0.03	<0.03	μg/L	p&t gcms	5
Tetrachloromethane	<0.05	<0.05	μg/L	p&t gcms	N/A
Tetrahydrofuran	<1	<1	μg/L	p&t gcms	N/A

Table 5.   Field parameters and analytical results for an unfiltered surface-water sample collected from the unnamed tributary to Butler Creek adjacent to the former hospital landfill, Fort Gordon, Georgia, September 8, 2010.—Continued

[id , identification; USEPA NPDWS (*NSDWS*), United States Environmental Protection Agency National Primary Drinking Water Standard (*National Secondary Drinking Water Standard*); ---, no trip blank results; µS/cm, microsiemens per centimeters at 25 degrees Celsius; s.u., standard pH units; mg/L, milligrams per liter; °C, degrees Celsius; <, less than; E, estimated; mg/L, micrograms per liter; icp, inductively coupled plasma; cicp, cell inductively coupled plasma; ms, mass spectrometry; lle, liquid-liquid extraction; p&t, purge and trap; gcms, gas chromatography mass spectrometry; N/A, not applicable; pct, percent]

	Downstreamsite id. 332608082080400	Trip blank id. 332443082064600	Units	Method	USEPA NPDWS (*NSDWS*)
Volatile organic compounds					
Toluene	<0.02	<0.04	µg/L	p&t gcms	1,000
trans-1,2-Dichloroethylene	<0.02	<0.02	µg/L	p&t gcms	100
trans-1,3-Dichloropropene	<0.14	<0.14	µg/L	p&t gcms	N/A
trans-1,4-Dichloro-2-butene	<0.4	<0.4	µg/L	p&t gcms	N/A
Trichloroethylene	<0.02	<0.02	µg/L	p&t gcms	5
Trichlorofluoromethane	0.09	<0.08	µg/L	p&t gcms	N/A
Vinyl chloride	<0.1	<0.1	µg/L	p&t gcms	2
1,2-Dichloroethane-d4	126	132	pct	surrogate	N/A
1,4-Bromofluorobenzene	88.9	89	pct	surrogate	N/A
Toluene-d8	91	99	pct	surrogate	N/A
Semivolatile organic compounds					
1,2-Dichlorobenzene	<0.2	---	µg/L	lle gcms	N/A
1,3-Dichlorobenzene	<0.2	---	µg/L	lle gcms	N/A
1,4-Dichlorobenzene	<0.2	---	µg/L	lle gcms	N/A
1,2,4-Trichlorobenzene	<0.3	---	µg/L	lle gcms	N/A
1,2-Diphenylhydrazine	<0.3	---	µg/L	lle gcms	N/A
2,4,6-Trichlorophenol	<0.34	---	µg/L	lle gcms	N/A
2,4-Dichlorophenol	<0.36	---	µg/L	lle gcms	N/A
2,4-Dimethylphenol	<0.8	---	µg/L	lle gcms	N/A
2-Nitrophenol	<0.4	---	µg/L	lle gcms	N/A
2,4-Dinitrophenol	<1.4	---	µg/L	lle gcms	N/A
2,4-Dinitrotoluene	<0.56	---	µg/L	lle gcms	N/A
2,6-Dinitrotoluene	<0.4	---	µg/L	lle gcms	N/A
2-Chloronaphthalene	<0.16	---	µg/L	lle gcms	N/A
2-Chlorophenol	<0.26	---	µg/L	lle gcms	N/A
3,3-Dichlorobenzidine	<0.42	---	µg/L	lle gcms	N/A
4,6-Dinitro-2-methylphenol	<0.76	---	µg/L	lle gcms	N/A
4-Bromophenyl phenyl ether	<0.24	---	µg/L	lle gcms	N/A
4-Chloro-3-methylphenol	<0.55	---	µg/L	lle gcms	N/A
4-Chlorophenyl phenyl ether	<0.34	---	µg/L	lle gcms	N/A
4-Nitrophenol	<0.51	---	µg/L	lle gcms	N/A
Acenaphthene	<0.28	---	µg/L	lle gcms	N/A
Acenaphthylene	<0.3	---	µg/L	lle gcms	N/A
Anthracene	<0.39	---	µg/L	lle gcms	N/A
Benz[a]anthracene	<0.26	---	µg/L	lle gcms	N/A
Benzo[a]pyrene	<0.33	---	µg/L	lle gcms	0.2
Benzo[b]fluoranthene	<0.3	---	µg/L	lle gcms	N/A
Benzo[ghi]perylene	<0.38	---	µg/L	lle gcms	N/A

Table 5   35

Table 5.   Field parameters and analytical results for an unfiltered surface-water sample collected from the unnamed tributary to Butler Creek adjacent to the former hospital landfill, Fort Gordon, Georgia, September 8, 2010 September 9, 2010.—Continued

[id., identification; USEPA NPDWS (*NSDWS*), United States Environmental Protection Agency National Primary Drinking Water Standard (*National Secondary Drinking Water Standard*); ---, no trip blank results; mS/cm, microsiemens per centimeters at 25 degrees Celsius; s.u., standard pH units; mg/L, milligrams per liter; °C, degrees Celsius; <, less than; E, estimated; mg/L, micrograms per liter; icp, inductively coupled plasma; cicp, cell inductively coupled plasma; ms, mass spectrometry; lle, liquid-liquid extraction; p&t, purge and trap; gcms, gas chromatography mass spectrometry; N/A, not applicable; pct, percent]

	Downstream site id. 332608082080400	Trip blank id. 332443082064600	Units	Method	USEPA NPDWS (*NSDWS*)
Semivolatile organic compounds					
Benzo[k]fluoranthene	<0.3	---	µg/L	lle gcms	N/A
Bis(2-chloroethoxy)methane	<0.24	---	µg/L	lle gcms	N/A
Bis(2-chloroethyl)ether	<0.3	---	µg/L	lle gcms	N/A
Bis(2-chloroisopropyl)ether	<0.14	---	µg/L	lle gcms	N/A
Bis(2-ethylhexyl)phthalate	<2	---	µg/L	lle gcms	N/A
Butyl benzyl phthalate	<1.8	---	µg/L	lle gcms	N/A
Chrysene	<0.33	---	µg/L	lle gcms	N/A
Dibenz[a,h]anthracene	<0.42	---	µg/L	lle gcms	N/A
Diethyl phthalate	<0.61	---	µg/L	lle gcms	N/A
Dimethyl phthalate	<0.36	---	µg/L	lle gcms	N/A
Di-*normal*-butyl phthalate	<2	---	µg/L	lle gcms	N/A
Di-*normal*-octyl phthalate	<0.6	---	µg/L	lle gcms	N/A
Fluoranthene	E0.01	---	µg/L	lle gcms	N/A
Fluorene	<0.3	---	µg/L	lle gcms	N/A
Hexachlorobenzene	<0.3	---	µg/L	lle gcms	1
Hexachlorobutadiene	<0.24	---	µg/L	lle gcms	N/A
Hexachlorocyclopentadiene	<0.5	---	µg/L	lle gcms	50
Hexachloroethane	<0.24	---	µg/L	lle gcms	N/A
Indeno[1,2,3-cd]pyrene	<0.38	---	µg/L	lle gcms	N/A
Isophorone	E0.02	---	µg/L	lle gcms	N/A
Naphthalene	<0.22	---	µg/L	lle gcms	N/A
Nitrobenzene	<0.26	---	µg/L	lle gcms	N/A
normal-Nitrosodimethylamine	<0.24	---	µg/L	lle gcms	N/A
normal-Nitrosodi-*normal*-propylamine	<0.4	---	µg/L	lle gcms	N/A
normal-Nitrosodiphenylamine	<0.28	---	µg/L	lle gcms	N/A
Pentachlorophenol	<0.6	---	µg/L	lle gcms	1
Phenanthrene	<0.32	---	µg/L	lle gcms	N/A
Phenol	<0.3	---	µg/L	lle gcms	N/A
Pyrene	<0.35	---	µg/L	lle gcms	N/A
2,4,6-Tribromophenol	86	---	pct	surrogate	N/A
2-Fluorobiphenyl	78	---	pct	surrogate	N/A
2-Fluorophenol	66	---	pct	surrogate	N/A
Nitrobenzene-d5	87	---	pct	surrogate	N/A
Phenol-d5	51	---	pct	surrogate	N/A
Terphenyl-d14	74	---	pct	surrogate	N/A